Contemporary Theatre
in Education

Contemporary Theatre in Education

Roger Wooster

intellect Bristol, UK / Chicago, USA

First Published in the UK in 2007 by
Intellect Books, PO Box 862, Bristol BS99 1DE, UK

First Published in the USA in 2007 by
Intellect Books, The University of Chicago Press, 1427
E. 60th Street, Chicago, IL 60637, USA

A catalogue record for this book is available from the British Library

ISBN 978-1-84150-170-3
Cover Design: Gabriel Solomons
Copy Editor: Holly Spradling
Typesetting: Planman Technologies

Printed and bound by Gutenberg Press Ltd., Malta.

For my parents and for my children,
Emily and Blake.

Contents

Acknowledgements

I would like to thank those TIE directors who agreed to talk to me about their work with young people and for giving permission to publish the transcripts of the interviews: Tim Baker and Jane Meakin from Clwyd Young People's Theatre, Ian Yeoman from Theatr Powys, Steve Davies from Spectacle Theatre, Kevin Lewis from Theatr Iolo, Geinor Jones and Rachel Clancy from Theatr Na n'Og, Iola Ynyr from Cwmni'r Frân Wen, Gary Meredith and Jain Boon from Gwent Theatre and Chris Cooper from Big Brum TIE.

My gratitude also goes to all the performers and other artists who were involved in the projects I visited. Thank you for your openness in allowing me to view your programmes and your friendly response to having an observer in the space whilst you were working.

At Trinity College Carmarthen, where this project was first engendered, I would like to acknowledge the advice, support and guidance of Kevin Matherick and, also, Roger Maidment and Jim McCarthy. Additional thanks to Charmian Savill for her helpful suggestions in preparing the final manuscript.

Thanks also to my children, Emily and Blake, who have been supportive, understanding and patient throughout my preoccupation with this project.

Chapter One

Introduction

It is generally accepted that TIE[1] emerged as a distinct 'hybrid' of theatre and education forms in 1965 with the work of the *Belgrade Theatre*, Coventry. This company began working in a unique way, using theatre and performance with small cohorts of children in schools, and involving these audiences as participants within the drama. Theatrically the lineage can be seen as coming from such genres as 'agitprop' and community theatre where it was felt pertinent to take theatre out of its usual hallowed environment and transpose it to places where a wider audience might have access and benefit. Underlying this was a socio-political belief that theatre needed to be democratized and made relevant to all social groups. The subject matter of such theatre thus tended to be socially and politically derived with a specific audience or message in mind. Simultaneously British theatre was experimenting more and more confidently with non-traditional and creative forms. The ideas of Brecht were gaining in popularity amongst actors and directors for the creative freedom and political integrity they offered. The 1960s witnessed a seminal change in social and personal liberty and many theatre practitioners preferred to work outside the confines of the traditional artistic and financial theatre structures.

Simultaneously, there was an increasing belief in the centrality of the child within education. Perhaps as a result of the deprivations of war, the generation growing up in the 1950s and 1960s demanded more from schools than mere preparation for work. Unrestricted by notions of a centrally defined curriculum, this demand was responded to by an increasing number of teachers interested in heuristic educational approaches. 'Progressive' educational ideas, that can be traced back to Rousseau, were now being accepted by many teachers, educational theorists and even governments. In Britain this progressive strand in education had been growing in strength since the beginning of the twentieth century. In the field of drama it is especially to be seen in the work of Harriet Finlay-Johnson, Caldwell Cook and then, post-war, in the work of Peter Slade, Brian Way and Dorothy Heathcote. These new educational priorities sought to place the child at the centre of their own learning. It was believed that more effective learning took place when children were encouraged to investigate the world through play and through active approaches to discovery. Group and project work, it was believed, would teach them to cooperate and understand the world both rationally and emotionally. This approach, often referred to as being 'child-centred', prioritized the child's emotional needs over the mere requirement to absorb knowledge and facts. Such ideas were never universally accepted and it would be perfidious to suggest otherwise, but this undercurrent gave the new subject of 'drama' a certain primacy. Within drama it was possible for children to address their personal and social needs, often within the wider demands of the [as yet undefined] curriculum.

Slade, Way and later Heathcote all recognized in drama and dramatic play the opportunity for children to come to terms with their own selves and the world. By using role play and reflection they were encouraged to find their place on their own world stage. Indeed, many drama theorists regarded this subject as having the potential to be at the centre of the education system, offering opportunities for cross-curriculum work and allowing for meaning-making within a holistic approach to learning.

Theatre in Education developed as a hybrid of these new theatrical and educational undercurrents and created a methodology that offered a child-centred approach to learning within a theatrical context. Christine Redington[2] has identified the quiddities of Theatre in Education as including child-centred learning, the use of play, learning by doing, project teaching and the use of drama in education techniques. She also maintains that projects should have an identified age group and include problem solving and language development. From theatre she sees the utilization of techniques of creative theatrical forms derived from Brecht's 'Epic' theatre using both empathy and objectivity to encourage the involvement of audience as critical observers.[3] The next chapter explores the degree to which this attempted fusion of emotional engagement and critical detachment became accepted as a defining characteristic of TIE by commentators in the twenty years following 1965.

The 'progressive' idea of encouraging children to think, to question and to challenge inevitably led to the work of both DIE[4] teachers and TIE actor/teachers coming under suspicion and subsequent threat. The whole concept of child-centred learning was increasingly being questioned during the 1970s and such approaches found themselves being blamed for social disquiet and industrial disharmony. The post-war educational consensus can be seen to have been breaking down at this time and, with the election of a Conservative government in 1979, it was clear that accepted educational theory was going to come under scrutiny.

The concept of a 'National Curriculum' was not originally part of the plans for this educational overhaul, but by the time of the Education Reform Act [1988] the necessity and value of such an entity had been widely accepted by those on the political right. A subsequent change of government [1997] indicated that this consensus had spread across the political spectrum since there has been no indication of a willingness to challenge the notion of a centrally directed National Curriculum. The Curriculum for the first time set out the 'Learning Objectives' for a defined range of subjects within each of four 'Key Stages'. The effect of this was to discourage project work and cross-curriculum approaches. More importantly to DIE and TIE was that drama was not accorded a place in the new

Curriculum and was instead subsumed within English. This clearly offered a major challenge to drama and TIE in schools which was to some degree ameliorated by the insistence of the Curriculum that children should have access to professional theatre and that they should develop both skills of artistic analysis of product and also performance and devising skills. This preserved the presence of drama in Key Stages 1–3, though the emphasis had fallen on theatricality and play making rather than drama. However, another strand of the National Curriculum has offered a second lifeline to those schools who wish to employ drama methodologies, for there are many references to the need for personal and social development. The Personal Social and Health Education [PSHE] curriculum has allowed many drama teachers to exercise their skills in this area. At the same time, however, training in drama at teacher training colleges has seen a sharp decline and the availability of the particular skills of the drama teacher are less present in schools.

It will be examined, in Chapter Four, how the Education Reform Act [ERA] may have offered both threats and opportunities to TIE. As with DIE, its working methods might not fit easily into the strictures of the Learning Objectives and Key Stages of the Curriculum, whilst the requirement for theatre form to be part of a child's education could also guarantee that there would be a demand for theatre within education. The stipulation that schools should access professional work could be offering touring TIE companies a security of patronage. It will be interesting to note whether there has been pressure to fulfil the curriculum delivery needs of schools in order to gain access to scarce time with pupils, and to identify whether such needs were at odds with TIE's function and perceived benefits. Such pressure might come not only from the Curriculum, but also from the Local Management of Schools [LMS], also part of ERA, which delegated budgets from Local Education Authorities [LEA] to schools. There has been potential for pressure upon TIE companies not only from curriculum needs, but also financially, for without centralized LEA support many companies have found themselves without reliable core funding.

In Wales, as will be shown, TIE has been more strongly nurtured by the artistic establishment, possibly because of the advantage of having a range of small touring companies as a means of creating theatrical arts provision in a predominantly rural country. These particular circumstances will be examined in Chapter Five. Despite the TIE companies going through the same change in environment as their English counterparts, the situation is, in 2004, that each of the counties of Wales has its dedicated TIE team. These are still generally funded by partnership arrangements between Local Authorities and the Arts Council of Wales [ACW], though most companies also make charges to schools. Unlike the situation in England, though some companies have disappeared or been amalgamated, all parts of Wales have had some continuity

Theatr Mewn Addysg yng Nghymru.

of service. In 1998, the newly devolved Welsh Assembly found itself with control of the arts and education budgets, and this, perhaps, has also allowed TIE to thrive in Wales as compared to England. This generally positive approach to TIE has not been without its tribulations, and this chapter also examines the TIE review [1998–2003] that at one point threatened to completely change the nature of theatre in education in Wales.

The question arising from the offered definitions of TIE and the political, educational and financial pressures is the extent that TIE in Wales [or in Britain generally] has been able to hold onto its drama roots and keep the defining characteristics of TIE as outlined by Redington and others. If TIE in Wales has managed to continue to provide a TIE service to children and schools, how has it done so? Wales still has a National Curriculum [though there are areas in which Welsh national requirements have been reflected] and teachers are under at least as much pressure to deliver a wide range of Learning Objectives, often in two languages.

In order to investigate the current form/s of TIE in Wales and to note any changes in educational philosophy, in the summer term of 2004 each of the eight companies in Wales was visited. Where available, the associated teaching materials were analysed and a member of the company was interviewed about the programme's content, approaches and methodologies.[5] The aim was thus to find out how and why TIE has managed to survive in Wales. Through studying the programmes and through interviews with directors, it was intended to determine the current form of TIE in Wales, whether the genre is surviving, and to note whether the original precepts of TIE are surviving the changes in the educational, financial and artistic environment. The information thus derived may serve as offering models and warnings to TIE wherever it is employed.

It should be expected that any art form, and indeed any educational approach, will be subject to healthy developmental forces. The relation between theatre and education was evolving during the 1960s and 1970s as the individual elements developed and created new ways of maximizing the potential of their symbiosis. The techniques being used by companies in the late 1970s, drawn perhaps from Heathcote and Boal, would be distinct from the Slade and Way derived approaches of early *Belgrade* programmes. However, the centrality and needs of the child were a defining aspect of this genre that became known as the 'TIE movement'. Through this study of TIE in Wales, it is intended to establish whether this evolution has continued from its genesis, and to discover whether contemporary TIE continues to give primacy to the needs of the child whilst having found ways of working within the constraints of the National Curriculum.

From the productions and the responses to the interviews it has been possible to make some broad observations and to draw some general conclusions about the current format and philosophy of TIE in Wales. However, the author is aware of the dangers of attempting to create a definitive classification of methodologies and policies from this one *tranche* of work. For example, few of the programmes visited contained extensive workshop elements, but many directors indicated that other programmes may contain more substantial involvement, dependant upon the perceived needs of the project and the target group.

Throughout this work a Darwinian metaphor has been employed which I hope the reader will not find too laboured. The argument is that a new 'species' evolved through the symbiosis of theatre and drama education techniques. Having defined the characteristics of this new species in the early chapters, this study proceeds to consider the extent to which these characteristics still identify work that is being called Theatre in Education. In Chapter Five the work of the Wales companies is analysed with a view to identifying these developments and considering the 'genetics' of the evolution of TIE. It may be that TIE has evolved to fulfil its unique potential in the new educational environment. However, it is also possible that the companies' work has become so distinct from former TIE form that a 'mutation' may be regarded as having taken place. The final chapter seeks to draw conclusions about the current state of TIE in Wales and to identify whether TIE still exists as a distinct form, or whether a new term might more properly be coined.

Notes

1. Theatre in Education.
2. REDINGTON, C. *Can Theatre Teach?* Oxford, Pergamon Press, 1983.
3. Ibid., p. 3ff.
4. Drama in Education.
5. See Appendix Three.

Chapter Two

The Origin of the Species: The Genetic Legacy from Drama in Education

The development of Theatre in Education [TIE] in Britain since the mid 1960s and in Wales from 1972 has been closely interwoven with Drama in Education [DIE] praxis. Before proceeding to analyse current TIE praxis in Wales it will therefore be appropriate to critically evaluate the methodological and philosophical approaches underpinning DIE which informed the development of this genre and to arrive at a definition of TIE against which current practice can be measured. DIE approaches that have affected TIE have included a recognition of the value of play, the ability of drama to encourage social and personal development and the use of 'role' and 'reflection'. To these TIE adds influences from theatre practice, especially Brecht but also the 1960s phenomena of 'alternative' theatre and agitprop.   *dylanwad pwysig.*

This chapter will first set out to investigate the common theoretical roots of DIE and TIE and consider some definitions. It will be argued that TIE's genesis was facilitated by particular educational and theatrical epistemologies of the 1960s within a post-war social context. However, in measuring current practice against an agreed definition, it will become essential to consider the changes in the educational hegemony within which TIE operates. It will then become possible to judge whether TIE is evolving to meet the needs of education and society, or whether it has mutated into something distinct from TIE. Has the demarcation, once so clear, between Children's Theatre and TIE become blurred, or redefined, or simply irrelevant, by the twenty-first century?

During the twentieth century, drama's value within the education system was increasingly appreciated. The pioneering work of unconventional educationalists such as Harriet Finlay-Johnson[1] and Caldwell Cook[2] offered approaches to drama practise within education that became increasingly valued by teachers and the inspectorate. Hodgson and Banham [1972] have offered a useful summary of the growing acceptance of drama within a school's curriculum.[3] They point out that it was only from 1919 that English was given primacy in the curriculum and that, within English, drama was seen to have a potentially powerful role. Drama had the power to help in the development of speech, movement and confidence. Further it was endowed with the ability to help the less able, and to serve as a cross-curricula tool. Hodgson and Banham note that, by 1940, drama was credited with giving an 'opportunity for each child to develop to the full his mental and physical resources'.[4] By 1950 'improvisation' was acknowledged as a useful tool in drama and there was 'the first consideration of the special role of the teacher as an encourager', a person who is 'a provider of ideas and stimulus rather than pedant or authority'.[5] An HMI document of 1949 notes that 'the development of the personality of the child, his growth as a whole, demand greater attention than the three "R"'s'.[6] In Wales, the Ministry of Education report of 1954 records that exploration through drama is 'one of the essential ways of learning' enabling the children 'to master their own little worlds'.[7] HMI reports of the 1960s define drama's potential with creditable insight, noting that it is 'a subject which enables children to experience, in play, emotions and ideas that otherwise are not safely available to them.'[8]

Here we see one of the earliest definitions of the power of DIE [and later TIE] to offer a safe context for 'reflection'. Through what was to become known as 'social drama' the DIE teacher was seen to contribute to 'solving particular and "special" problems'.[9] As will be shown, enabling young people to understand their world and empowering them to act in their world, was a central tenet of drama and TIE from the 1960s until the 1990s, and as late as 1993 Wooland argues that 'drama is a social art form; it is concerned with how individuals relate to the world they live in…'.[10]

This rapid development in the status of drama within education can be seen as part of the 'progressive education' movement that grew up following the Second World War. The Education Act of 1944 ostensibly recast education in Britain as a universal system offering opportunity to all sectors of society. In retrospect this can be seen as entrenching class divisions through a 'tripartite' system that offered academic or technical training alongside a basic education for those likely to enter unskilled occupations. This system, still regarded as a paradigm by some, was largely superseded by Comprehensive schools from 1976. Prior to this, and then within the tripartite system, 'progressive education' of which drama was a central part was taking a hold.

It is argued that the context for these 'progressive ideas' within education is part of the wider social change of the 1950s and 1960s. It may be easily understood that following the privations of their own economically depressed childhoods, a World War that decimated many families, and the hardships of post-war reconstruction and continuing rationing, parents during this period were predisposed to seek a happier and freer childhood for their own children. The 1950s saw the growth of a youth culture as the result of increasing disposable incomes for the young and the development of a consumer society. The 1960s and 1970s witnessed a growth in liberalization which both reflected changes in personal relationships and engendered further changes. In 1961 the Pill was introduced to Britain and in 1964 the first Brook Clinic was set up[11]; the first Abortion Act was passed in 1967 followed by a reform of the divorce laws in 1969. Alongside these reforms affecting relationships came the abolition of

cymdeithas wedi newid

yn gyflym.

theatre censorship [1968], the Equal Pay Act [1970] and the Sex Discrimination Act [1975]. Within a generation of the end of the Second World War, British society had been transformed. In primary schools, and to an extent in the 'tripartite' secondary schools, new educational theories were responding to this transformed social context.

Particularly in the primary schools, the focus was on 'child-centred' learning. Ken Jones[12] characterizes this approach as viewing children 'as unique individuals; learning was the product of the active relationship between individuals and the environment'.[13] The approach was characterized by a light-handed approach to discipline and a broad curriculum with a belief in creativity and emotional development; education was not just about preparation for work,[14] but rather about the 'development of an individual's capabilities'.[15] This approach was sanctioned and championed by the Newsom and Plowden Reports.[16] The Newsom Report especially acknowledges the place that the arts should have in the school curriculum, helping young people 'to come to terms with themselves more surely than by any other route,' and enabling them 'to work out their own personal problems'.[17]

'Child-centred' and 'self-discovery' concepts of education drawn from Rousseau's *Emile* by Froebel, Pestalozzi and Dewey, now seemed to have a place in the curriculum. Finlay-Johnson was clearly echoing Rousseau when she wrote that 'childhood should be a time for absorbing big stores of sunshine for possible future dark times.'[18] The prescience of these words is disturbing, since many of her pupils were to lose their lives in the World War that broke out three years later. With the increased validity offered by Piaget's work on child developmental psychology, the usefulness and indeed the necessity of play and 'discovery' become firmly embedded in child education. Alington was an early drama proponent of 'child-centred' education:

> Education is only inadvertently a 'preparation for life'; it is chiefly the fulfilment of the present.[19]

pwysigrwydd
plentyndod

Central to this educational approach was the importance given to children's play and a belief that 'nature would have children be children before being men.'[20] There was an acceptance that 'play' is a central part of being human and that through play we learn and develop both motor skills and psychological well-being. This tenet underpins DIE and TIE theory.

Peter Brook, in his influential work *The Empty Space*, notes enigmatically that 'a play is play'.[21] He is pointing out that the human facility to play both enables the theatrical art form to exist and provides the technical foundation for what actors do. This is not to say, as some have argued, that the only purpose of drama is theatre. The ability to 'play' is a pre-requisite of theatre but it is also a building block for continuing human and personal development. Drama,

[handwritten margin note: Cysylltiad theatre, chwarae, o addysg]

'playing', enables us to be the architects of our own construction. This is rooted in a post-war understanding of child psychology. Mary Lowenfold writes extensively about the importance of play to a young child, which she described as 'a perpetual endeavour to check up experience with reality… to grasp what reality is really like.'[22] The importance of this is clearly reflected in the progressive educational ideas of Illich,[23] Richmond,[24] Head,[25] and Postman and Weingartner.[26] Perhaps the best-known progressive educationalist in Britain has been A. S. Neill, who maintains that 'the fundamentals [of play] are in the hearts of all children and all races.'[27] He continues:

[handwritten margin note: plant heddiw?]

When a child has lost the ability to play, he is psychologically dead.[28]

[handwritten note: A.S Neill]

Interestingly, however, this realization did not lead to Neill using drama as part of his pedagogic approaches. His references to drama are exclusively theatrically orientated and based around the performance of plays and sketches that were written by himself for the entertainment of the school.

The theorists whose ideas have dominated drama as a subject between 1955 and 1985, and so influenced TIE, have all recognized the importance of play and the fact that whilst opening the portal to the art form of theatre, it is also a key feature of the process of human learning. Play is part of being human and, according to Davis, 'the power of theatre to humanise' has been a central precept of TIE philosophy.[29] Alington points out that 'play is a necessity for man; children learn and develop through play.'[30] R. M. Jones notes that 'children must sometimes imagine reality the better to test it.'[31]

Discovery through play was thus linked to the potential for humans to change and conceive of change. As such, it became an important feature of DIE/TIE. O'Toole recognizes TIE as being 'an extension of children's play' utilizing 'a combination of theatricality and classroom technique.'[32]. Barker, who uses 'play' as the touchstone of his training of actors, has identified how it is part of the human learning process:

[Through games] we experience, we objectivise what we have learned from experience or reflection, we consciously decide to change; we reprogramme the mechanism to react in the light of that decision the next time we meet a similar situation.[33]

Therefore, despite the increasing utilitarianism of education at the turn of the twentieth century, the value of play was still recognized,[34] and it is still acknowledged that drama 'contributes to pupils' personal, social, moral and spiritual development.'[35]

The discovery of 'self' and the investigation of the world through play led to a diminishing of the importance of performance as part of the drama process.

Indeed, Peter Slade maintains that 'audience is often the enemy of the moment.'[36] It can be argued that modern drama education theory was instigated by Slade, and perhaps the most distinctive contribution he makes is the 'anti-theatrical' approach which separates him from Cook and Finlay-Johnson. In his developing theory of 'Child Drama', which Slade regards as 'a high Art Form in its own right',[37] we can recognize a distinct use of drama, aside from theatrical production, which was to set the agenda for Way, Heathcote and Bolton and for the TIE companies that took up their ideas.[38] The focus of drama was not to be theatrical production but self-awareness:

> The Drama is often used for playing out situations in which the individual has to make decisions about morals. By making situations conscious, the child is able to look at life as an observer and make slow inward decisions.[39]

The purpose of Child Drama was to 'create happy and balanced individuals'.[40] In this way, Slade is also affirming values of drama which were to be developed by those working in psychology. He was clear, however, that the crucial function of his work was 'not actually a therapeutic one, *but the even more constructive one of prevention.*'[41] In *Freedom in Education* he remarks that 'education of the emotions and behaviour is a veritable screaming need of our age.'[42] Even some thirty years later it is hard to disagree. Allen is less convinced by Slade's approach, describing 'Child Drama' as 'a kind of loosely organised dramatic play that children devise when left to themselves.'[43]

The value of drama as a tool for personal development was further investigated by Brian Way. In his seminal work *Development Through Drama* he argues for 'genuine emotional training'[44] using drama. He was clearly developing the philosophy of Slade with further emphasis on the social and psychological value of drama to the child and the 'individuality of the individual'.[45] Like Slade, Way is claiming a central role for drama within education:

> Drama in Primary Schools is not a subject… but a method of, or an aid to teaching.[46]

His contemporary, Richard Courteney, stresses the point, claiming that 'drama is a way of looking at education as a whole… It demands that we re-examine our whole education system.'[47] For Way, drama is part of 'emotional training aimed at helping educate a young person to become fully responsible for control of his own behaviour.'[48] It was 'a positive way of developing all aspects of an individual's personality.'[49]

The response to the development of this kind of drama work by HMI continued to be supportive and appreciative:

Beth ddylai drama fod (handwritten marginalia)

> The claim that drama can contribute to self-discipline, personal and emotional development and human relationships, has been substantiated by much of the admirable work we have seen.[50]

At the time of the Education Reform Act of 1988, the Gulbenkian Report for the Arts Council of Great Britain [ACGB] also felt it necessary to champion this argument by maintaining that the absence of arts education 'is simply to fail to educate them as fully developed, intelligent and feeling human beings.'[51] The report claims that 'the purposes of education include moral purposes,'[52] and this would be one aspect of the report with which drama and TIE practitioners would agree.

The key mechanism for this personal education drew on the ability for one human being to empathize with another, 'to know how it feels to be in someone else's shoes'.[53] This facility, obviously used by actors, was increasingly exploited by drama theoreticians within the safety of role play. The value of 'role' in drama education was becoming increasingly accepted and admired. The Schools Council Report [1977] applauded the use of role which allowed 'the children to distance themselves from the issue whilst allowing them the opportunity of expressing themselves through the characters.'[54] The DES document "Drama 5-16" [1989] declares on its opening page that 'drama in schools... relies on the human ability to pretend to be someone else';[55] a tacit acceptance that, even with the imminent arrival of the National Curriculum, role play was still recognized as a useful drama activity. The document also recognizes the value of drama in assisting pupils to 'face intellectual, physical, social and emotional challenges'.[56] The value of role is largely related to the licence it offers those involved to reflect upon the situations within which it is being used. Clearly derived from the human propensity to 'play', it is an aspect of drama which, as 'Dorothy Heathcote reminds us... is not something special, but rather a technique most ordinary people regularly employ as a way of coping with new or unsettling experience.'[57] Ross echoes the point:

> We are all actors. We all make dramatic use of ourselves to represent our experience to others.[58]

For Heathcote, Bolton and for the TIE practitioners who adapted their work, the use of role allows safe engagement with the issues in a 'no penalty zone'.[59] In this way, the fear of failure, which Holt identifies as one of the greatest bars to education,[60] can be avoided. Way has also identified drama's ability to achieve this, noting that 'through drama it is possible to try out "what happens if...?"'[61] whilst Courtney remarked that 'drama is involved in all educational purposes... in the form of trying out the affairs of life'.[62] Perhaps adapting Brecht's notion of the 'spectator' as opposed to 'audience', Bolton suggests that the self-spectatorship of role 'protects the participants into a level of emotion from which they may remain safely detached, both *engaged* and *detached.*'[63] Fleming usefully designates those involved in drama in this way 'percipients'.[64] Hodgson found a connection between the safety of role and the original work of Caldwell Cook:

> ...the drama room is a kind of laboratory of life where things can be tried out with control and safety.[65]

In Heathcote's developing theory the notion of role developed into increasingly demanding models of practice through which the children would come to discover 'what they already know but don't yet know that they know'.[66] Most famous of these is Mantle of The Expert [which 'changes both who you are and who your class are'[67]], but these were later followed by the Enterprise and Commission models. All of these require the children to work within role, maintaining critical and objective detachment. In Mantle of the Expert *'the fictional starting point will rarely be that of the matter being studied'*[68] but for TIE companies the use of role is different and a 'frame' or 'holding form' is often determined prior to the involvement of the children. Both, however, use role and participation. Heathcote aimed to develop emotional maturity through role and this was lauded by the 1977 Schools Council Report.[69] In Heathcote's use of role, issues can be examined without the burden of responsibility. Holt notes that children often see themselves as stupid because they are treated as such by adults:[70]

> We don't have to *make* human beings smart. They are born smart. All we have to do is *stop* doing the things that make them stupid.[71]

Heathcote's praxis, adapted by TIE, acknowledges this truth. Further, we are allowed 'to stand back and see what it is that we are experiencing.'[72] O'Toole expresses the experience of the child thus: 'this is happening to me *and* I am making it happen'.[73] He thus neatly summarizes that unique quality of being emotionally engaged whilst maintaining an objective control and detachment. For Heathcote, participatory role also gives the children 'the power to influence, not only to watch'.[74] The effect is similar in TIE. The children are 'aware that the person in role is role-playing (i.e. not "for real").'[75] Role is thus employing the same 'willing suspension of disbelief' as is required by theatre. The audience/spectators/participants are not only receiving verbal messages but also reading what Heathcote called 'signs':[76]

> Non-verbal signs are particularly powerful. Children are expert at non-verbal signals.[77]

Dangos nid dweud

This enables children to be engaged in the drama without being directly 'told'. It is an empowering use of human body language that encourages children to respond, and to respond with consideration and thought.

Another central notion of drama education from the mid 1970s was the use of 'reflection'. The Schools Council Report [1977] maintained that 'everyone needs moments to rest, reflect and evaluate.'[78] This might sound a somewhat soporific process, but in drama it involves stopping the action to allow consideration of motivations and thus to reflect on the universal implications of the particular situation being explored. Heathcote pointed out that 'to deal with something... by looking at it sideways on is always going in the long run to get you much, much nearer.'[79] For Heathcote, and for the developing TIE praxis, 'dramatic activity was concerned with the crises, the turning points of life, large and small, which cause people to reflect and take note.'[80] Facilitation of reflection became a key purpose of DIE, and DIE theory within TIE; to slow down action and thought processes to allow analysis and consideration of consequences. The theatrical dimension of such an approach allows us, in the words of the South American socialist dramaturgist Augusto Boal, 'to imagine variations' of our actions[81] and allows a metaxis where we are in a 'state of belonging completely and simultaneously to two different autonomous worlds'.[82] We can *be* and *observe ourselves being* at the same time. The power of role is augmented within a TIE programme to empower children 'to arrest the drama, stop it, analyse the drama... To find out what was motivating people... [to create] a dialectic between the cognitive and the emotional.'[83]

The purpose of 'reflection', in Heathcotian terms, is to access the 'universals' of human existence and to be able to relate one's experience within the drama to universal aspects of that same experience. In this way personal feelings are validated, justified and contextualized.[84] Traditional education can be about 'finding your place in the world', but, as Witkin points out, 'if the price of finding oneself in the world is that of losing the world in yourself, then the price is more than anyone can afford.'[85] The value of Heathcote's developments in role and frame is that 'her pupils are given a safe "feeling" context in which to consider "universal" concepts.'[86] Deriving 'universals' from particular events or symbols was especially important to TIE theory as practised in the 1980s because the 'dropping of a particular into the universal is the digestion process of the arts, which creates the opportunity for reflection which is what education is all about'.[87]

Thus, reflection 'is a metacognitive activity'.[88] It is the means by which students begin to understand how they learn. It was this opportunity for reflection, within role or 'frame' that became a defining characteristic of Theatre in Education as opposed to Children's Theatre. Evolving TIE theory, from the 1960s through to the late 1980s, regarded this participatory opportunity for the 'audience' to reflect upon the issues of the drama as central to its work. It

wysighwydd

dlewyrchu

dadansoddi

offered a quality of education 'which cannot be brought about in other ways' and which 'can enable children to think hypothetically about other people'.[89]

In DIE it was generally accepted, prior to ERA, that the *process* of drama held the key to its value. As we have witnessed, Slade, Way and Heathcote all eschewed drama as 'performance'. The emphasis, using role and reflection, was on the process rather than the product, or, as Caldwell Cook had maintained, 'not for the destination but for the journey'.[90] In the 1980s Boal's ideas of Forum and Image Theatre found their way into DIE and TIE practice and explored the use of highly subjective reflection as opposed to the 'universals' offered for analysis by Heathcotian approaches. Participants were encouraged to consider, through role play, how to overcome perceived oppressions in their own lives. For Boal, the act of analysing and considering the issues is the first step to resolution:

It is more important to achieve a good debate than a good solution.[91]

Boal was very much at one with the British drama theorists who sought to use drama to test out ideas rather than portray or present them. His approach has a resonance with Heathcote's, for she notes that children should be able to 'test out their ideas, try them over again and generally exercise them'.[92] In *The Theatre of the Oppressed*[93] and throughout his subsequent work, Boal maintains that the function of drama 'should be the initiation of changes the culmination of which is not the aesthetic phenomenon but real life'.[94] Once again, the learning process of drama rather than any aesthetic product is being emphasized. Interestingly, Slade had already anticipated Boal's use of therapeutic drama, for in the 1950s he noted that he liked to:

… reverse role… so as to begin to build up sympathy [for others].[95]

Later work by Heathcote and Bolton reveals a similar train of thought with the development of 'incipient role play' where participants are encouraged to 'envisage the future'.[96] In his introduction to Boal's "The Rainbow of Desire", Jackson noted the use of a 'difficultator' [as opposed to a 'facilitator'] to reinforce on a group the complexity of a situation,[97] whereas in traditional theatre situations 'the audience is de-activated, reduced to contemplation'.[98] Again there is an empathy here with Heathcote, for as Wagner relates, 'reflection is the only thing that in the long run changes anybody'.[99] In this manner, a common feature of TIE in the 1970s and 1980s became the use of an actor/teacher as 'facilitator', working sometimes in role, sometimes as teacher and sometimes as actor.

Augusto Boal was thus a further strong influence upon DIE/TIE, defining still more closely the uses of drama to empower participants to reflect upon their own condition with a view to enabling change. This was a power 'uniquely possessed by human beings – and not by animals – to observe themselves in action.'[100] Again we see the stress being laid upon the power of drama to be a humanizing influence and the potential of drama to facilitate change, for if the participants in drama 'don't change the world, no-one will change it for them'.[101]

The belief that education and the arts could be a mechanism for individual change runs through DIE and associated TIE theory. Personal change implicitly suggests associated social change and it was this aspect of drama and TIE that at times caused friction within the education system. Whilst personal development could usually be applauded as an educational aim, the pursuance of social change is fraught with danger. As will be shown, in TIE this facilitation of challenge, and the consideration of change, was derived as much from theatrical influences as from drama:

[Theatre should be] 'not just to explain the world but also to change it'.[102]

Similarly, Johnson and O'Neill referred to drama as aiming to 'build a path for change',[103] whilst for Robinson, the focus of social education, as part of DIE, is about helping the children 'to understand and reflect on the social values which are pressing on them, and their part in the dialectics of change.'[104] However, this change may not be a mere external reality; for Jackson the 'richness of classroom drama lies in its potential to achieve a change of understanding'.[105] Heathcote summarized it thus:

Drama is about shattering the human experience into a new understanding.[106]

If drama has the power to achieve this, as many would claim, then drama, and TIE using drama, is crucial, for 'to be adapted in his environment the individual must be able to act effectively as an integrated person.'[107] A great deal of responsibility is being placed here upon drama. It is a responsibility that was also present in *theatrical* ideas popular in the developing TIE movement. Muir, in discussing Brecht, explains that 'theatre should explore causes and effects and demonstrate through the simultaneous presentation of alternatives the possibility for change.'[108] Similarly, Boal's use of drama is about facilitating change and contributing 'to the preparation *of* the future rather than waiting for it to happen.'[109] TIE employs this metaxis of feeling and reflection to facilitate change within the minds of children and to help them make sense of their world. From understanding, it is thought, will proceed the possibility to create change in the children's objective realities.

In this way the purpose of drama, in the minds of many theorists and teachers, was to help children make sense of the world in which they live and to empower them:

Drama is about making meaning.[110]

The desire to enable children to make sense of themselves and the world around them can be discerned in the ideas of Slade and Way. Robinson indicates that the main value of drama in schools was 'as a form of social education'.[111] Bolton recognizes a similar capacity in Heathcote's work, where DIE 'harnesses make-believe's natural capacity for meaning indicating.'[112] In the face of demands for theatre-centred drama education he later asserted that 'talent is not the issue, the making of meaning is.'[113] Again this leads both DIE and TIE into controversial areas, for the value and advisability of encouraging children to question is not universally accepted. O'Toole points out that 'dramatic meanings are always social meanings'[114] but in society's efforts to preserve the innocence of childhood, it is something that is often mistrusted. Ken Byron puts the case firmly, and in a way that TIE companies of the 1970s and 1980s would applaud:

> The drama teacher's function is to assist young people to engage with the world in which they live.[115]

For O'Toole, DIE has an advantage over TIE, for the TIE team 'do not have the luxury of the drama teacher to construe and re-construe the meaning [of symbols] with audiences.'[116] However, it is arguable whether drama teachers often have the luxury of time to do this well, and whether a well-constructed TIE participatory programme might not indeed attain this objective. For Bolton, the case is clear; 'drama is for understanding – this is its purpose.'[117] The combination of seeking understanding and facilitating change clearly has a political dimension. Itzin has pointed out that 'all theatre is political[118] and to this we shall return in Chapter Four, after a consideration of the theatrical environment in which TIE was engendered.

Notes

1. FINLAY-JOHNSON, H. *The Dramatic Method of Teaching*, London, Nisbet, 1911.
2. COOK, H. Caldwell, *The Play Way*, London, Heinemann, 1917.
3. HODGSON J. & BANHAM M. *Drama in Education 1, Annual Survey*, London, Pitman, 1972.
4. Ibid., p. 21.
5. Ibid., p. 23.
6. MINISTRY OF EDUCATION, *Story of a School*, London, HMSO, 1949, p. 9.
7. MINISTRY OF EDUCATION, *Drama in the Schools of Wales*, London HMSO, 1954, p. 2.
8. HODGSON J. & BANHAM M. (1972), op. cit., p. 26.
9. Ibid., p. 27.
10. WOOLLAND, B. *The Teaching of Drama in the Primary School*, London, Longman, 1993, p. 9.
11. Brook Clinics offer family planning advice.

12. JONES, K. *Education in Britain 1944 to the Present*, Cambridge, Blackwell, 2003, p. 54.
13. Ibid., p. 54.
14. Ibid., p. 54.
15. Ibid., p. 55.
16. MINISTRY OF EDUCATION, *Half Our Future, The Newsom Report* London, HMSO, 1963. DEPARTMENT OF EDUCATION AND SCIENCE, *Children and their Primary Schools*, [The Plowden Report] London, HMSO, 1967.
17. MINISTRY OF EDUCATION (1963), op. cit., p. 157.
18. FINLAY-JOHNSON, H. (1911), op. cit., p. 27.
19. ALINGTON, A. F. *Drama and Education*, Oxford, Blackwell, 1961, p. 29.
20. LESTER SMITH, W. O. *Education*, Harmondsworth, Penguin, 1957 p. 39.
21. BROOK, P. *The Empty Space*, London, Penguin, 1968, p. 157.
22. LOWENFELD, M. *Play in Childhood*, Bath, Gollanz, 1969, p. 184.
23. ILLICH, I. *Deschooling Society*, Harmondsworth, Penguin, 1973.
24. RICHMOND, W. K. *The Free School*, London, Methuen, 1973.
25. HEAD, D. (ed.), *Free Way to Learning*, Harmondsworth, Penguin, 1974.
26. POSTMAN N. & WEINGARTNER C. *Teaching as a Subversive Activity*, Harmondsworth, Penguin, 1969.
27. NEILL, A. S. *Summerhill*, Harmondsworth, Pelican, 1968, p. 67.
28. Ibid., p. 69.
29. DAVIS, D. "Geoff Gillham", obituary in *The Guardian*, 27/7/01, London, Guardian, 2001.
30. ALINGTON, A. F. (1961), op. cit., p. 14.
31. JONES, R. M. *Fantasy and Feeling in Education*, Harmondsworth, Penguin, 1972, p. 22.
32. O'TOOLE, J. *Theatre in Education*, Hodder and Stoughton, London, 1976, p. vii.
33. BARKER, C. *Theatre Games*, London, Methuen, 1977, p. 21.
34. See, for example, NATIONAL ADVISORY COMMITTEE ON CREATIVE AND CULTURAL EDUCATION, *All Our Futures*, Sudbury, DFEE, 1999, pp. 29–30.
35. OFSTED, *The Arts Inspected*, Oxford, Heinemann, 1998, p. 45.
36. SLADE, P. *Child Drama*, London, Hodder & Stoughton, 1954, p. 49.
37. Ibid., p. 68.
38. Slade foresaw the creation of the profession of Actor/Teacher in 1954, ibid., p. 272.
39. Ibid., p. 73.
40. Ibid., p. 105.
41. Ibid., p. 119.
42. SLADE, P. *Freedom in Education?* Birmingham, Educational Drama Association, (date unknown) p. 6.

43. ALLEN, J. *Drama in Schools: its Theory and Practice*, London-Exeter, Heinemann, 1979, p. 13.
44. WAY, B. *Development Through Drama*, London, Longman, 1967, p. 237.
45. Ibid., p. 3.
46. Ibid., p. 5.
47. COURTNEY, R. *Play, Drama and Thought*, London, Cassell, 1968, p. 57.
48. WAY, B. (1967), op. cit., p. 158.
49. Ibid., p. 160.
50. DEPARTMENT OF EDUCATION AND SCIENCE, *Drama: Education Survey 2*, London, HSMO, 1967, p. 107.
51. CALOUSTE GULBENKIAN FOUNDATION [Revised Edition], *The Arts in Schools*, London, Calouste Gulbenkian Foundation, 1989, p. 19.
52. Ibid., p. 20.
53. HEATHCOTE, D. "Role Taking" in JOHNSON, L. & O'NEILL, C. [eds], *Dorothy Heathcote: Collected Writings*, London, Hutchinson, 1984, p. 49.
54. MCGREGOR, L., TATE, M. & ROBINSON, K. *Learning Through Drama. Report of Schools Council Drama Teaching Project 10–16*, London, University of London Press, 1977, p. 57.
55. DEPARTMENT OF EDUCATION AND SCIENCE, *Drama 5–16*, London, HMSO, 1989, p. 1.
56. Ibid., p. 1.
57. WAGNER, B. J. *Dorothy Heathcote: Drama as a Learning Medium*, London, Hutchinson, 1979, pp. 15–16.
58. ROSS, M. *The Creative Arts*, London, Heinemann, 1978, p. 75.
59. A phrase that Heathcote frequently uses. See, for example, HEATHCOTE, D. "Signs (and Portents?) – the use of role for actors" in *SCYPT Journal* no. 9, London, SCYPT, 1982, p. 23 and HEATHCOTE, D. "Material for Significance" in L. JOHNSON & C. O'NEILL (1984) *Dorothy Heathcote: Collected Writings*, London, Hutchinson, 1984, p. 129.
60. HOLT, J. *How Children Fail*, Harmondsworth, Penguin, 1984, p. 71.
61. WAY, B. op. cit., p. 178.
62. COURTNEY, R. op. cit., p. 54.
63. BOLTON, G. *Acting in Classroom Drama*, Stoke on Trent, Trentham Books, 1998, p. 200.
64. FLEMING, M. *The Art of Drama Teaching*, London, David Fulton, 1995, p. 2.
65. HODGSON, J. & BANHAM, M. op. cit., p. 129.
66. WAGNER, B. J. op. cit., p. 13.
67. BOLTON, G. & HEATHCOTE, D. *So You Want to Use Role Play?* Stoke on Trent, Trentham, 1999, p. 122.
68. BOLTON, G. *Acting in Classroom Drama*, Stoke on Trent, Trentham Books, 1998, p. 241.
69. MCGREGOR, L., TATE, M. & ROBINSON, K. op. cit.

70. HOLT, J. op. cit., p. 80.

71. Ibid., p. 161.

72. HEATHCOTE, D. "Material for Meaning in Drama", *London Drama*, vol. 6, no. 2, 1980, p. 7.

73. O'TOOLE, J. *The Process of Drama*, London, Routledge, 1992, p. 98.

74. HEATHCOTE, D. "Signs (and Portents?) – the use of role for actors", op. cit., p. 26.

75. LAWRENCE, C. "Teacher and Role – a drama teaching partnership", in K. BYRON (ed.), *DramaDance 2D*, vol. 1, no. 2, Leicester, 2D, 1962, p. 8.

76. HEATHCOTE, Dorothy (1982), op. cit.,

77. LAWRENCE, C. op. cit., p. 17.

78. MCGREGOR, L., TATE, M. & ROBINSON, K. op. cit., p. 65.

79. HEATHCOTE, D. "Moving into the Drama" in *SCYPT Journal 13*, London, SCYPT, 1984, p. 23.

80. HEATHCOTE, D. *Drama Activity*, reprinted in Liz JOHNSON & Cecily O'NEILL (1984), *Dorothy Heathcote: Collected Writings*, London, Hutchinson, 1969, p. 55.

81. BOAL, A. [trans. Adrian Jackson], *The Rainbow of Desire*, London, Routledge, 1995, p. 13.

82. Ibid., p. 43.

83. Interview with Louise Osborn, 10th June 2003, Llandrindod.

84. See, for example, HEATHCOTE, D. "From the Particular to the Universal" in K. ROBINSON (ed.), (1980), *Exploring Theatre and Education*, London, Heinemann, 1980.

85. WITKIN, R. W. *The Intelligence of Feeling*, London, Heinemann, 1974, p. 1.

86. WOOSTER, R. "Emotional Involvement or Critical Detachment" in *DRAMA*, vol. 11, no. 2, Glasgow, National Drama, 2004, p. 19.

87. BYRON, K. "Drama at the Crossroads, Part Two" *DramaDance 2D*, vol. 7, no. 1, 1987, p. 11.

88. MORGAN, N. & SAXTON, J. "Dorothy Heathcote: Educating the Intuition" in *Broadsheet. The Drama Education Journal*, vol. 11, 1995, p. 14.

89. MCGREGOR, L., TATE, M. & ROBINSON, K. op. cit., p. 209.

90. COOK, H. Caldwell, op. cit., p. 8.

91. BOAL, A. [trans. Adrian Jackson], *Games for Actors and Non Actors*, London, Routledge, 1992, p. 230.

92. HEATHCOTE, D. "Material for Meaning in Drama" in *London Drama*, vol. 6, no. 2, 1980, p. 7.

93. BOAL, A. [trans. Adrian Jackson], *Theatre of the Oppressed*, London, Pluto Press, 1979.

94. BOAL, A. (1992), op. cit., p. 245.

95. SLADE, P. *Experience of Spontaneity*, London, University of London Press, 1958, p. 225.

96. BOLTON, G. & HEATHCOTE, D. (1999), op. cit., p. 25.

97. BOAL, A. (1995), op. cit., p. xix.
98. Ibid., p. 41.
99. WAGNER, B. J. op. cit., p. 77.
100. BOAL, A. (1992), op. cit., p. xxvi.
101. Ibid., p. 21.
102. WILLETT, J. *Brecht on Theatre*, London, Methuen, 1964, p. 72.
103. JOHNSON, L. & O'NEILL, C. op. cit., p. 12.
104. ROBINSON, K. (ed.), op. cit., p. 175.
105. JACKSON, T. *Learning Through Theatre*, London, Routledge, 1993, p. 39.
106. HEATHCOTE, D. "Drama as a process for Change" (1976) in R. DRAIN, *Twentieth Century Theatre*, London, Routledge, 1995, p. 122.
107. WITKIN, R. W. op. cit., p. 28.
108. MUIR, A. *New Beginnings*, Stoke-on-Trent, Trentham, 1996, p. 8.
109. BOAL, A. (1995), op. cit., p. 185.
110. HEATHCOTE, D. & BOLTON, G. *Drama for Learning*, Portsmouth, New Hampshire, Heinemann, 1995, p. 4.
111. ROBINSON, K. (ed.), op. cit., p. 141.
112. BOLTON (1988), op. cit., p. 176.
113. HEATHCOTE, D. & BOLTON, G. (1995), op. cit., p. 4.
114. O'TOOLE, J. (1992), op. cit., p. 13.
115. BYRON, K. "Drama at the Crossroads, Part Two" in *DramaDance 2D*, vol. 7, no. 1, 1987, p. 10.
116. O'TOOLE, J. (1992), op. cit., p. 43.
117. BOLTON, G. "Theatre Form in Drama Teaching" in K. ROBINSON, op. cit., p. 71.
118. ITZIN, C. *Stages in the Revolution: Political Theatre since 1968*, London, Methuen, 1980, p. x.

Chapter Three

The Origin of the Species: The Theatrical Legacy and the Theatre and Education Hybrid

Craig maintains that the emergence of TIE was part of the 'alternative theatre' movement of the 1960s.[1] Following the innovations of Becket, Pinter and Osborne in traditional theatre spaces of the 1950s, and the influx of ideas from Brecht and Artaud, there was a desire to forge new form in Britain. Coult regards TIE as 'a true inheritor of Brecht's political aesthetics,'[2] whilst Craig maintains that this new theatre, uniquely amongst the arts of the 1970s, identified itself with the plight of the oppressed.[3] John McGrath's *7:84* company is a clear example of this. Developing work from a socialist perspective, McGrath avoided theatre buildings and sought to build up a working-class audience in clubs and community centres using techniques developed from music hall and folk traditions.[4] Craig argued that key to the philosophies of alternative theatre was a desire to widen the audience base, a perspective shared by Gill Ogden. Ogden, considering Welsh TIE, suggests that the work be seen as part of the anti-elitist theatre of the 1960s, along with community, alternative and agitprop theatre, 'embracing the idea that theatre can and should be performed anywhere, at any time…'.[5] This, she asserts led to a desire to take theatre into schools developing child-centred learning and 'the use of drama as a learning tool.'[6] Indeed, she feels that 'the wide range of style and emphases in TIE in Wales have contributed some of the most innovative and dynamic experimental theatre in the country in the last ten years.'[7] O'Toole also sees TIE as part of 'fringe theatre' with its emphasis on ensemble performance, co-devising, polemical purpose and targeted audience,[8] whilst Itzin, in her analysis of revolutionary theatre, declares that the significant theatre of Britain from 1968 to 1978 was that of political change.[9]

Brechtian theatrical ideas, both political and technical, were a key feature of TIE performance style. Bolton frequently points out that drama teachers are able to make the ordinary seem extraordinary. This is very similar to Brecht's requirement that his actors should note where 'they were astonished in reading the script' for at those points the spectators should 'also be astonished'.[10] From Brecht also comes the use of 'depiction' or 'gestus', much used for purposes of reflection in DIE and TIE. Indeed, the whole premise of Brecht's work is to encourage thought and analysis and to inspire action in his 'spectators'. Like many TIE companies, Brecht would mistrust distanced emotional catharsis unless it was reinforced by an opportunity to identify potential for change. Further, Brecht's preferred style of acting, 'demonstrating', and keeping a

Gwleidyddiaeth a Theatr Mewn Addysg.

detachment from the character played, informed much of the work of TIE companies in both their acting style and in the adaptation of role to suit participatory workshop elements of programmes. From Brecht, TIE actors would 'demonstrate their knowledge of human relations, of human behaviour, of human capacities.'[11]

As part of the 'alternative theatre' genre, TIE was also perceived, not unfairly, to share its radical politics. The politics of the late 1960s were characterized by student rebellion, alternative lifestyles and CND, and radical art played an active role in these events. The power, the *responsibility*, of artists to effect change was recognized. As Craig puts it, theatre is 'forced continually to decide in whose service it acts.'[12] For this reason, TIE along with agitprop theatre and McGrath's political/community theatre were viewed with suspicion by the establishment.

Thus, by the late 1960s, there was a body of radical drama theory emerging from the education sector in Britain and this coincided with the development of alternative concepts of theatre. However, unlike most alternative theatre, which can survive on the good will and passion of its artists, TIE also requires a significant resource infrastructure and liaison with schools. If, as Itzen maintains, TIE 'developed in the wake of widespread politicisation and raising of political consciousness at the end of the sixties'[13], then how did this radicalism come to be accepted into schools? Tony Coult offers one explanation. In the 1960s, he asserts, there was a 'brief collision of national affluence and educational idealism.'[14] When one considers that educational idealism has been replaced by educational utilitarianism, and that financial restraints seem to have affected both arts and education continually since the mid 1970s, we should perhaps be not a little surprised that we still have any TIE in British schools.

The reaction to this education/theatre hybrid was initially, and understandably, cautious. Woolgar [1971] expresses the feeling that even actor/teachers with teaching experience 'must to some extent be inadequate because they don't know the children well enough',[15] and he reports comments from a conference group that 'it was unsatisfactory for Professional Theatre Groups to go into schools and give drama lessons'. Furthermore, were it to happen, then 'teachers should be trusted to choose the right children to be used.'[16] One discussion group even questioned the 'compatibility' of drama and theatre 'in an educational context.'[17] Unhappily, these were comments from drama specialists.

Wariness from head teachers is perhaps to be more expected [though the SHA report of 1998[18] does much to dispel this idea]. The Schools Council Working Paper on Arts and the Adolescent [1975] reports that heads seemed to have little concept of the function of the arts in education which were generally seen as 'spare time activities' especially suited to lower ability groups.[19] Ross also notes the perennial problem of 'the rival claims of "theatre studies" and participation'.[20] Implicitly he identifies the roots of this conflict:

> Subject knowing is *subject-reflexive action: feeling impulse* projected through an *expressive medium* yields *feeling form.*[21]

Thus, Drama in Education was developing the power of drama to encourage thought, reflection and analysis in young people. Theatre in Education was able further to exploit this access to 'feeling form' through combining the DIE methodology with theatrical technique. The conception of TIE can be seen as the product of a particular moment in educational, theatrical and social history. Historical and social factors, developments in the arts and education, all co-reliant, combined to provide the environmental conditions in which a new species could emerge. Ideas of progressive education, new concepts of the theatre arts and social liberalization facilitated the creation of this new form of theatre/education which, by the 1970s, was becoming highly sophisticated and theoretically mature. Yeoman acknowledges the debt to DIE:

> Theatre in Education practice over the last number of years has been hugely informed by the theoretical developments made in drama teaching.[22]

As has been indicated TIE was learning from DIE the power of play, role, reflection and meaning-making. What TIE was able to add to this mix, from the world of theatre, was a portrayal of the objective world and the way in which people operate in that world:

> The full power of drama can be realised only when the inner world of meaning is connected to the outer world of expressive action.[23]

Warner here indicates the powerful sphere in which TIE operates. Theatre practitioners with an interest in education were able to straddle the two worlds and create the powerful praxis of TIE that demands the 'physical, emotional and intellectual involvement of the participants.'[24] In a TIE project it can be useful for children to observe emotions being played prior to analysing them within role. They thus avoid being allowed to just 'wallow' in the catharsis and they are not expected to engage in any emotional exposure of themselves. This approach offers an 'immediacy of concern' which is a 'primary cause of energy surges in learning'.[25] 'Feelings are both a *vehicle towards* understanding and *an expression* of understanding.'[26] Thus, TIE is not about training feelings but understanding feelings. It is about internalizing an understanding of moral issues.[27] Robinson tends towards a belief in the primacy of theatre as an effective conveyor of symbols:

> In theatre, the division between actors and audience means that the distinction between the real and the symbolic levels of understanding is… clear.[28]

He goes on to point out, though, that in a drama lesson 'there is both a symbolic and a real interaction between all of the participants simultaneously.'[29] Here again we see how TIE can actually exploit both the strengths of theatre *and* drama education by allowing the children to perceive the symbolism objectively *and* through feeling when involved in a participatory fashion. O'Toole maintains that educational drama essentially uses the children's innate ability to play and role-play as a means of deepening and making more efficient the process of learning. TIE adds to this the dimension of presentation and a sense of audience.[30] Drama and TIE use 'the symbolic representation at first hand of the working out of relationships involving human beings' and 'there are no consequences'.[31]

Schweitzer states the mechanics of TIE as creating an interest [through theatre] and then placing the child 'in a situation where he has to use that interest... to some avail.'[32] The involvement of children in this way has often been carried out in TIE projects via a 'simulation'. Linnell defines TIE simulations as 'a way of setting up a collection of circumstances that will be as near to reality as possible, whilst still retaining the safeguards of a manufactured or unreal situation'.[33] Here the clear influence of Heathcote's models can be seen. The children are not required to perform. Murphy states the distinction succinctly:

The children don't act: they are themselves within assumed roles.[34]

For Heathcote, her work 'does not take the place of theatre-orientated work... It uses the same laws'.[35] Indeed, it is the heady mixture of challenging theatre and drama practice that makes TIE a uniquely valuable pedagogic tool, for 'when actors create a situation which contains the *necessity* for the kids to deal with a real problem, then something really takes place.'[36] Bolton has analysed the links between DIE and TIE praxis. He points out that, as in drama, participants in TIE are not expected to 'act' but only 'to be'. They are involved in a 'process orientated' experience in a 'living through' mode. 'They are the agents as well as the recipients of the experience.'[37] Importantly, Bolton maintains that 'DIE and TIE share the same goals'.[38] Amongst these goals is that of meeting and solving problems.

As TIE developed, it increasingly redefined for itself the theoretical legacy bequeathed by DIE. Largely through the work of the *Standing Conference of Young People's Theatre* [SCYPT], established in 1976, TIE praxis developed independently. Through an annual conference and through its journal, SCYPT encouraged debate on educational priorities and critical analyses of TIE programmes. The debate was often passionate and highly politicized. It is often argued that it has been the role of Bolton to give a theoretical frame to the DIE praxis of the 1970s and 1980s, interpreting and codifying the sometimes opaque work of Heathcote.[39] It can be argued that SCYPT fulfilled the same function for TIE. Redington has pointed out that 'TIE does not support the status quo, but questions society and demands changes'.[40] She credits SCYPT with encouraging companies to address basic educational issues; 'What is it important to know? What do children learn? What should they learn? and How do they learn?'[41] As with drama, the focus is on developing social awareness and humanity in the safe environment of protected role or frame. From Heathcote's 'no penalty zone' was drawn the idea that TIE 'can offer children a challenge in a context where being wrong is not relevant.'[42] TIE uses 'theatrical elements [as] a means not an end.'[43] The methods are drawn from theories of play, learning by doing, discovery, meaning-making [through role and reflection], problem solving, games and simulations. Theatrically there is use of plot, conflict, characters, empathy and often technical aids. Specifically Brecht's ideas of 'spectating', 'demonstrating' and 'alienation' have been adapted, as has Boal's use of role to 'rehearse' future change. SCYPT was the portal through which these ideas reached the TIE movement and gave it a much-needed theoretical backbone. But SCYPT also exposed TIE to accusations of political bias.

Boal states that 'all problems are political'.[44] Thus, in dealing with 'problems', personal or social, TIE always ran the risk of being seen as political. This was a threat to both DIE and TIE. It is a paradox, that at a time when society was overtly becoming more liberal, the implications of encouraging young people to think and to challenge accepted ideas was in many areas disapproved of. Pammenter points out that 'it is useful to challenge accepted truth… as part of the process of enabling the child to discover his or her responses.'[45] Even the ACGB notes with approval that drama has the power to develop 'the practice of critical reflection'.[46] The TIE companies were aware that 'empowering' children could be seen as revolutionary and that, at the very least, questioning implied a challenge to the status quo. As the committee of the SCYPT Journal points out in 1995, theatre and drama 'hold the means to explore the central questions which face humanity'.[47] Boal notes that though 'the cops are in our head… their headquarters and barracks must be on the outside',[48] whilst O'Toole feels that 'TIE has been intensely and explicitly political since the late 1960s, much more so than the bulk of drama in education.'[49] Baskerville states that TIE is political because 'it has to be a mouthpiece which communicates values'.[50] Certainly, when exploring social [and by implication] political issues, the actor/teacher has a great responsibility not to exploit the position of power with which they are endowed by virtue of being an 'exciting' visitor to a school. Schweitzer hints at this problem thus:

> TIE is an art form as well as an educational tool and the artist must not only state, but move towards resolving, moral and political dilemmas; not didactically, but through careful manipulation of the audience's sympathy for particular characters at particular moments.[51]

Into the educational debate in the 1970s came the influential work of Freire, *The Pedagogy of the Oppressed*. This work gave a new and politicized energy to progressive and left-wing educationalists who were invited to consider that 'just as social reality exists not by chance, but as an product of human action, so it is not transformed by chance.'[52] Clearly such concepts were of interest to socially aware teachers and actor/teachers either directly, or through Boal's work, itself inspired by Freire. Chief among Freire's criticisms of current educational hegemony was that education had become 'an act of depositing' information and that true learning was not taking place.[53] These theories had resonance for both TIE and DIE where 'authentic teaching' [to use a Heathcote phrase] was deemed to be central to their approaches. Freire wanted, as did TIE and DIE, to create situations:

> [where we can] resolve the contradiction between teacher and student… in a situation in which both address their act of cognition to the object by which they are mediated.[54]

In TIE this 'object' was the drama or theatre stimulus around which the programme was created. Within a few years of *Coventry Belgrade*'s tentative experiments with drama and theatre, and through the guidance of SCYPT from 1976, TIE had developed in ways which could be neither identified as 'pure theatre' nor 'pure education'. Coult characterizes the TIE hybrid as being 'performed by professionals, experienced and/or trained in both theatre and teaching techniques'.[55] He goes on to identify the defining feature of TIE thus:

> TIE's characteristic formal device, and an actual innovation in theatre technique, is some form of active participation by the audience.[56]

That definition was published in 1980 as was Pam Schweitzer's observation that 'participation is part of a tight programme structure.'[57] The HMI survey of TIE in Wales [1989] identifies TIE in a similar fashion and notes that the actors will provide 'some kind of participatory experience for the pupils'.[58] Clearly, participation has been regarded as a key component of TIE, but all definitions must be treated with caution, for times and circumstances change. The earlier definition [1975], from Eileen Murphy, has clear links with Heathcote and DIE, but cannot comfortably be applied to many excellent TIE programmes of the 1980s:

> A group of actors, in character, and a group of children… exploring and living through a situation in which they are physically and emotionally involved.[59]

Conversely, some definitions have stressed the educational component without insisting on participatory elements. Redington [1983] points out that theatrical elements of TIE are a means to an educational end[60] and distinguishes TIE from Children's Theatre which, she maintains, 'can, and frequently does happen in a vacuum' and does not provide 'a satisfactory educational resource'.[61] Jackson [1993] writes that the distinctive feature of TIE is that it 'seeks to harness the techniques and imaginative potency of theatre in the service of education,'[62] though he also seeks to point out that 'the key distinguishing feature [of TIE is] the participatory format'.[63] It is clear that a universal definition of TIE is not easy to identify. There are those who will insist upon the active participation of the children whilst others will be satisfied if the theatrical event has an educational goal.

Notes

1. CRAIG, S. (ed.), *Dreams and Deconstructions: Alternative theatre in Britain*, Ambergate, Amber Lane Press, 1980.
2. Ibid., p. 76.
3. Ibid., p. 9.
4. McGRATH, J. *A Good Night Out*, London, Eyre Methuen, 1981.
5. OGDEN, G. in A-M. TAYLOR (ed.), *Staging Wales*, Cardiff, University of Wales Press, 1997.
6. Ibid., p. 48.
7. Ibid., p. 57.
8. O'TOOLE, J. (1992), op. cit., p. 11.
9. ITZIN, C. op. cit., p. x.
10. BESSEL, R. *Brecht on Stage*, BBC Open University, 1994.
11. WILLETT, J. *The Theatre of Bertolt Brecht*, London, Methuen, 1977, p. 26.
12. CRAIG, S. op. cit., p. 30.
13. ITZIN, C. op. cit., p. xii.
14. COULT, T. "Agents of the Future" in S. CRAIG, op. cit., p. 76.
15. WOOLGAR, M. "The Professional Theatre in and For Schools" in N. DODD & W. HICKSON (eds) *Drama and Theatre in Education*, London, Heinemann, 1971, p. 91.
16. Ibid., p. 110.
17. Ibid., p. 123.
18. SECONDARY HEADS ASSOCIATION, *Drama Sets You Free*, Bristol, Central Press, 1998.
19. ROSS, M. *Schools Council Working Paper 54, Arts and the adolescent*, London, Evans/Methuen, 1975, p. 12.
20. Ibid., p. 51.
21. Ibid., p. 57.
22. YEOMAN, I. "The Actor's Role" in *SCYPT Journal 30*, Lancaster, SCYPT, 1995, p. 28.

23. WARNER, C. "The Edging in of Engagement" in *Research in Drama Education*, vol. 2, no. 1, 1997, p. 22.
24. HENNESSEY, J. "The Theatre in Education Actor as Researcher" in *Research in Drama Education*, vol. 3, no. 1, 1998, p. 87.
25. ARMSTRONG-MILLS, C. in D. DAVIS, *Interactive Research in Drama in Education*, Stoke on Trent, Trentham Books, 1997, p. 101.
26. ALLEN, G., ALLEN, I. & DALRYMPLE, L. "Ideology, Practice and Evaluation: developing the effectiveness of Theatre in Education" in *Research in Drama Education*, vol. 4, no. 1, 1999, p. 29.
27. Ibid., p. 30.
28. ROBINSON, K. op. cit., p. 164.
29. Ibid., p. 164.
30. O'TOOLE, J., (1976), op. cit., p. 18.
31. Ibid., p. 19.
32. SCHWEITZER, P. (ed.), *Theatre-in-Education: Four Secondary Programmes*, London, Methuen, 1980, p. 8.
33. LINNELL, R. in SCHWEITZER ibid., p. 156.
34. MURPHY, E. introduction to Bolton Octagon Theatre-in-Education Company, *Sweetie Pie*, London, Methuen, 1975, p. 7.
35. HEATHCOTE, D. & BOLTON, G. *Drama for Learning*, Portsmouth, New Hampshire, Heinemann, 1995, p. 194.
36. BASKERVILLE, R. "Theatre in Education" (1973) reprinted in *SCYPT Journal 13*, London, SCYPT, 1984, p. 11.
37. BOLTON, G. "Drama in education and TIE: a comparison" in *Selected Writings*, Harlow, Longman, 1986, p. 181.
38. Ibid., p. 184.
39. See, for example, BOLTON, G. *Towards a Theory of Drama in Education*, London, Longman, 1979.
40. REDINGTON, C. *Can Theatre Teach?* Oxford, Pergamon Press, 1983, p. 22.
41. Ibid., p. 119.
42. Ibid., p. 212.
43. Ibid., p. 2.
44. BOAL, A. (1995), op. cit., p. 4.
45. PAMMENTER, D. in T. JACKSON, *Learning Through Theatre*, London, Routledge, 1993, p. 63.
46. ARTS COUNCIL OF GREAT BRITAIN, *Guidance on Drama Education*, London, ACGB, 1992, p. 5.
47. SCYPT Journal 30, Lancaster, SCYPT, 1995, p. 5.
48. BOAL, A. (1995), op. cit., p. 8.
49. O'TOOLE, J. (1992), op. cit., p. 46.
50. BASKERVILLE, R. op. cit., p. 10.
51. SCHWEITZER, P. (ed.), op. cit., p. 13.
52. FREIRE, P. *Pedagogy of the Oppressed*, Harmondsworth, Penguin, 1972, p. 27.

53. Ibid., p. 45.
54. Ibid., p. 65.
55. COULT, T. in S. CRAIG, op. cit., p. 76.
56. Ibid., p. 80.
57. SCHWEITZER, P. (ed.), op. cit., p. 11.
58. H. M. I., A Survey of Theatre in Education in Wales, Cardiff, Welsh Office, 1989, p. 1.
59. MURPHY, E. op. cit., p. 5.
60. REDINGTON, C. op. cit., p. 2.
61. Ibid., p. 94.
62. JACKSON, T. op. cit., p. 1.
63. Ibid., p. 26.

Chapter Four
The Fight for Survival

Even in the 1960s, at the same time that this philosophy of 'child-centred learning' was being developed by educationalists and the embryonic TIE movement, the philosophy was being challenged. The supposed excesses of 'progressive education' were increasingly being identified, led by the reactionary trumpetings of the 'Black Papers':

> Influenced by a variety of psychologists from Freud to Piaget, as well as by educational pioneers from Froebel onwards... schools have increasingly swung away from the notion... that education exists to fit certain sorts of people for certain sorts of jobs... to the idea that people should develop in their own way at their own pace.[1]

Such arguments arguably set Callaghan's mind on its philosophical route to his Ruskin College speech in 1976. The 'Great Debate' on education which followed can be seen as leading to the Tory educational reforms of 1988.

These reforms were a response to a general disenchantment with post-war educational ideas. Liberal educationalists were blamed for all the country's social and economic ills and the old order was to be replaced by a system which could produce the skills the country needed. The Education Reform Act 1988 [ERA] sought to sweep away the progressive and non-utilitarian ideas of which TIE/DIE had been a hotbed. Clutty [1992] identifies an increasing antipathy to perceived politicization of aspects of the schools' curriculum including 'peace studies' and CND, and an accompanying drive to teach about enterprise and profit.[2]

Within the context of this study, two aspects of ERA are worthy of particular note since they impacted directly upon TIE companies. The first of these was the Local Management of Schools [LMS] which transferred a large element of budgetary control from Local Authorities to individual schools. The result of this was to place great pressure on all peripatetic services, including TIE, since individual schools would now have to decide whether to include within their budgets the cost of TIE or whether to spend allocations on more 'parent-sensitive' resources such as books and teachers. There was no mechanism for groups of schools to 'commission' work from TIE companies whose incomes became depleted, erratic or non-existent. Many companies disappeared in the years after LMS, preferring to do so rather than charge schools.[3]

The other major effect of ERA was the introduction of the first National Curriculum that significantly affected both TIE and DIE. Drama was not granted 'core' status as part of the new arrangements and instead found itself embedded within English. It was given a key role in delivering aspects of literacy, speaking and listening and, alongside this, a role in the development of the study of theatre as an art form. The effect on drama in the classroom was quickly felt. The ACGB report of 1992 acknowledges that 'drama helps us make sense of the world',[4] but quickly goes on to stress the links with English, the importance of performance and presentation, the value to pupils with Special Educational Needs, and the fact that 'theatre is part of the entertainment industry'.[5] A similar process was happening in the history curriculum where emphasis on the learning of 'facts' was felt by many to be to the detriment of history's true value and based largely on the convenience of such an approach for assessment.[6] Overlooking the work of TIE during the past twenty-five years, the ACGB stresses the need for theatre visits and also for school plays.[7] Drama was crucial to the curriculum but it was about 'making, performing and responding.'[8] The effect on TIE companies was not immediate, but gradually they found themselves under pressure to offer work that matched the literacy [and/or the theatrical] Learning Objectives of the National Curriculum.

Those companies that were now having to charge schools for their services found themselves obliged to accept large 'audiences' to which they 'performed' educational drama pieces rather than TIE programmes in which participatory praxis could be utilized. This pressure had been present whenever financial pressures were being applied. Increasingly in the late 1980s and into the 1990s participation in TIE programmes was under threat. Yeoman noted in 1995:

> Current economics threaten the existence of this practice entirely.[9]

Elsewhere he remarks that ERA 'was the beginning of the end of our work'.[10] Theatre in Education was in danger of disappearing within a generation of becoming a highly valued resource:

> This then was the paradigm of the first twenty years of TIE; a free service to schools, working thoroughly and in depth with small groups, in liaison with teachers, providing an often high quality theatrical performance combined with deeply considered educational aims based on the work of trusted theorists.[11]

But, as Jackson succinctly puts it, TIE 'was quite a different animal' by 1993.[12] The threat to TIE was perhaps more a result of the financial pressures from LMS, but the praxis itself, as for DIE, was under pressure to change. From drama, TIE had inherited a strong child-centred philosophy; 'the absolute centrality of the child'.[13] Gillham, for example, maintains that 'children are capable of dealing with "difficult" and complex issues because they are living in this world, not in some other "world of the child"'.[14] Elsewhere he asserts that 'to develop the young as conscious social beings is to provide them with the knowledge and skills to act in accordance with the social requirements of living now and in the future.'[15]

However, it must be accepted that circumstances change. It is perhaps reasonable to expect that TIE will evolve to serve the developing needs of education and society. Redington points out that TIE teams have had 'to adapt to the circumstances... whilst retaining [their] central purpose.'[16] Since the 1970s these changes have included the 'abolition' of the 11+ Examination, the introduction of Comprehensive schools and experiments with cross-curricula and project work.[17] It has clearly been more difficult for TIE to adapt to the educational requirements of ERA, not only because of the apparent shift of educational policy to the political right, but also because, in Redington's analysis, by 1976 TIE companies were, in any case, seeing themselves as being outside the education system offering alternative ideas.[18] Companies were protective of their educational and political values and often companies with a coherent political commitment were producing the best work.[19] As will be seen later, a new argument was to emerge based on the question of where TIE's responsibility lay. Pammenter recognizes this dilemma for post-ERA TIE where the 'TIE teams have a responsibility to the education system but a greater responsibility to the children'.[20]

In the immediate post-ERA period some commentators were very aware of the dangers to TIE. Jackson, whose definition of TIE emphasized the 'structured active participation of the children',[21] notes the impact of ERA on TIE praxis, including the increased emphasis on theatre skills and the fact that the imperative for teachers is to be involved in the 'delivery of a narrowly conceived and examination-orientated National Curriculum.'[22] Readman notes that ERA was bound to cause changes in the relationship between schools and TIE companies.[23] He comments that

> Many primary schools are finding it difficult to tackle anything which is outside the National Curriculum and their curriculum planning is... in advance of timescales operated by many TIE companies.[24]

The National Curriculum cannot be avoided, and Readman asks whether companies can 'work outside the parameters of the ERA when all their clients are being compelled to implement it on a day-to-day basis?'[25] An additional aspect of ERA to which he draws to our attention, was the increased power given to the governing bodies of schools. This, along with LMS, has had the effect of giving the power over the provision of TIE to bodies with probably no experience and certainly little understanding of the genre.[26] In times of economic stringency – which always seem to be present – the danger to educational 'frills' is profound. Indeed, it may be easier, in this context, to market the idea of a performance 'treat' for the children rather than an additional educational experience. This may be another pressure on companies to turn to performance-based rather than participatory work. It appears that some twenty years after the appearance of the new TIE hybrid, political, financial and educational circumstances were conspiring to force mutation or even extinction.

Notes

1. COX, C. B. & DYSON, A. E. *Fight for Education, A Black Paper*, London, Critical Quarterly Society, 1969, p. 6.
2. CLUTTY, C. *Towards a New Education System: The Victory of the New Right*, Lewes, Falmer Press, 1992, p. 151.
3. Tag MacEntegert called the free service 'a proud ferocious tradition'. Interview 12th June 2003, Telford.
4. ARTS COUNCIL OF GREAT BRITAIN, *Guidance on Drama Education*, London, ACGB, 1992, p. 1.
5. Ibid., p. 3.
6. SLATER, J. in R. ALDRICH (ed.), *History in the National Curriculum*, London, Institute of Education, 1991, p. 38.
7. Ibid., p. 4.
8. Ibid., p. 5.
9. YEOMAN, I. "Acting in Role" in *SCYPT Journal 30*, Lancaster, SCYPT, 1995, p. 36.
10. YEOMAN, I. "SCYPT – a Perspective" in *SCYPT Journal 28*, Lancaster, SCYPT, 1994, p. 48.
11. WOOSTER, R. "Paradigm Lost?" in *The Journal for Drama in Education*, vol. 22, issue 1, Barnsley, NATD, 2006, p. 20.
12. JACKSON, T. op. cit., p. 2.
13. YEOMAN, I. (1994), op. cit., p. 49.
14. GILLHAM, G. "Unsuitable for Children" in SCYPT Journal 20, Porth, 1990, p. 21.
15. GILLHAM, G. "Notes on a Curriculum for Living" in *SCYPT Journal 30*, Lancaster, SCYPT, 1995, p. 49.
16. REDINGTON, C. op. cit., p. 103.
17. Ibid., p. 113.
18. Ibid., p. 118.
19. Ibid., p. 118.
20. PAMMENTER, D. in T. JACKSON, op. cit., p. 63.
21. JACKSON, T. ibid., pp. 1–2.

22. Ibid., p. 34.
23. READMAN, G. in T. JACKSON, ibid., p. 267.
24. Ibid., p. 272.
25. Ibid., p. 275.
26. Ibid., p. 273.

Chapter Five

The Welsh Environment

In Wales companies were facing similar challenges to the development of TIE praxis. There have also been particular circumstances relating to the governance of Wales and to distinct Arts policies that have offered different threats and opportunities. These are considered here in a separate chapter though many companies will recognize some or all of the issues analysed. In particular, many will recognize the way in which the pursuit of 'artistic excellence' and 'value for money' can be used to justify change that will guarantee neither, and may indeed be introduced with apparent wilful ignorance of that which is being appraised.

Wales saw its first company set up in 1972 some six years after Belgrade began their TIE work. By the late 1980s each county had a company that claimed to be producing TIE. As in England, the effects of ERA were significant. Ogden [1997] notes the continuing impact of the National Curriculum and Standard Assessment Tests and the increasing financial autonomy for schools. The low status of the arts and the fact that companies needed to charge schools for their work were also perceived threats, and Ogden felt that

> The general movement towards market-led forces and external economic forces may undermine the artistic and philosophical autonomy of TIE…[1]

The Arts Council of Wales' decision in 1998 to restructure TIE provision in Wales can be seen as an aspect of this economic and artistic pressure. Ogden's fears that there would be further moves to charge schools, to play to larger audiences with less participation and workshop elements, and to offer work based on set texts, all seemed to be well founded.

From the mid 1970s, it had been the policy of WAC [The Welsh Arts Council] to see a TIE company established in each of the counties of Wales. *The Breconshire Theatre Company* [later to become *Theatr Powys* after local government reorganization] was established in 1972 to be followed in 1976 by *Action Pie, Gwent Theatre, Open Cast Theatre* and *Spectacle*. In the late 1970s there was increasing pressure on companies to be able to operate bilingually. Within ten years, though companies had mutated and developed, changed their structures and their names, there was in Wales a 'sustained provision of TIE in both Welsh and English that was greater in scope and vision than anything elsewhere in the UK.'[2] By 1988 there were eight companies in Wales. Ten years later the renamed ACW [Arts Council of Wales] had decided that the status quo needed to be re-examined.

The motives behind the perceived need to restructure drama and theatre provision in Wales, as so often in such matters, were couched by the protagonists in terms of pursuing 'excellence'. To those affected, political and economic motives were suspected. Ruth Shade suggested that ACW was finding its level of commitments unsustainable due to government economic policies.[3] She saw the reduction in Welsh Office funding in 1996 and 1997, the reduction of Local Authority monies, a standstill Welsh Office subvention from Whitehall in 1998 and 1999 and the below-inflation ACW grant in 1999 and 2000, as being the drivers behind the need for a drama strategy. In 1998 the Arts Council of Wales published a consultation paper entitled "Building a Creative Society". Two thousand documents were distributed and twenty public meetings held throughout Wales. The Arts Council reported that 220 responses to the document were received.[4] The purpose of the paper and consultation was to 'develop a practical vision for the arts, following years of a reduction in ACW's own grant.'[5] According to ACW the pattern of eight TIE companies, based on the now defunct eight-county structure of Wales, was experiencing 'severe problems of sustainability'.[6]

In September 1998 ACW initiated specific consultation on Theatre for Young People which culminated in its *Draft Drama Strategy for Wales: Consultation Paper* in January 1999. The subsequent consultation showed, according to ACW, that change was welcomed 'particularly the need to fund fewer companies better'.[7] ACW reported that it received 151 responses and held 23 meetings.

In June 1999 the *Strategy* was published with the declaimed aim of addressing 'the need to support professional production of high artistic quality and the need to ensure access to that work across Wales'.[8] As part of this pursuit of quality, a new national framework 'to supply professional theatre tailored to young people' was proposed. This was to be achieved by inviting applications for five time-limited Funding Agreements to develop a *Young People's Theatre* network across Wales. The closing date for applications was September 1999 and guidelines and additional points of clarification 'were circulated to all parties understood to be interested in applying.'[9]

The ACW claimed that the five franchises were seen as an opportunity to prioritize funding to the economically deprived areas of Wales and to reflect the European constituency boundaries based on population. As a result three of the five companies would be based in the South Wales' valleys and the other two would cover Mid, North and West Wales. Funding for the new companies would reflect that given to the previous eight, though work not directed to young people would be removed from the equation. Thus, a company working within a combined TIE and community theatre brief would only have their schools or youth work considered.

In January 2000 the five franchises were announced as part of the wider *Strategy for Drama*. *The British Theatre Guide* summed up the proposals *vis-à-vis* TIE thus:

Theatr Powys representing the largest rural area in Wales has lost its grant completely; Theatre Gwent has had its territory ceded to a Cardiff based company, Theatr Iolo; Spectacle Theatre, based in the Rhondda, is the only company operating in the Valleys – the highest population density in the county: Arad Goch must cover twice its original area with less money.[10]

The article goes on to point out that, whilst the current reach of TIE companies was 111,000 children, the ACW's target under the new franchise arrangements was just 57,000. Following the announcement there were immediate representations from local government, politicians, the arts community and the public. Neither schools, Local Authorities nor national politicians were content. Even those Local Authorities whose companies had been awarded a coveted franchise were dissatisfied that 'their' company would now be expected to work outside 'their' area. Very often it was Local Authority monies that had set up and nurtured the companies and the action of ACW must have seemed to some to be something of a 'hostile takeover'. The vitriolic response to the Arts Council's action made national television and newspaper headlines. In the face of overwhelming opposition and 'possible legal challenges' there was a 'clear need to rethink'.[11] It was not only TIE and YPT that were to be affected. It was also proposed to remove funding from *Hijinx*, Wales' only company specializing in work for people with special needs. This did not accord well with the policies on inclusiveness, access and participation in the arts espoused by ACW and the Welsh National Assembly. There was widespread feeling that the process had been rushed, ill-conceived and badly researched. As a result of the resulting furore, the YPT element of the *Strategy* was suspended and funding for the existing eight companies was confirmed for the three years from 1 April 2000.

Ruth Shade saw the content of the *Drama Strategy* as altruistic artistic intention couched in 'a reactionary mode of thinking'.[12] She felt that ACW, like WAC before it, had difficulty in 'decolonising its mind'[13] and breaking away from preconceptions of what Welsh theatre should be, based upon English and ACGB expectations. This trait is observable in each of the periodic reviews that WAC/ACW have undertaken in their history. In 1966 a report concluded that 'well-equipped theatres are Wales's greatest need' in order to ensure that Wales should have access to a theatre tradition.[14] There was, maintained Shade, an assumption that no tradition of theatre existed in Wales that was not amateur or amateurish. In Shade's analysis, the proliferation of YPT and experimental companies should provide the model for future development but, faced with economic decisions, ACW is again turning towards English theatre models to justify a retraction of provision:

> When it faces a financial dilemma… the Arts Council meets the challenge in a predictable way: namely it secures the future of those ventures which most correspond with traditional concepts of 'quality'.[15]

She points out that from 1994 to 1999 the building-based *Clwyd Theatr Cymru* received an 111 per cent increase as against *Hijinx*'s 1.52 per cent.[16]

From the pace of the chronology outlined above it can be seen that ACW had seriously misjudged the situation within the TIE community and within the wider educational and public domain. With very little notice, long-established TIE companies were pitched into a situation in which they had to compete for funds and existence. They also had to draw up their plans and make their 'bids' with very little time and with a reluctance to accept the rules of the game being imposed upon them. There was no time to object or negotiate, for any delay might mean that their bid would be inadequate or even miss the deadline, making any future uncertain. They had to provide answers to some thirty questions and to offer 'evidence' for their future proposals in terms of artistic policy and educational excellence. The ideology of ACW presupposed a particular view of theatre and its function which companies were being forced to absorb and then demonstrate in their future plans. Despite the ACW's protestations that the process was about equity of provision and improved funding, it was clearly the case that companies prepared to engage in the process were to be involved in a 'Dutch auction'. The secret to securing a franchise was to offer a high level of coverage for a minimum cost. Under such circumstances it was highly unlikely that educational or artistic integrity would survive. Many saw the process as a cynical mechanism to reduce the number of companies and reduce expenditure in the medium and long term.

The effect on the companies was profound not just in artistic terms. Firstly, they had to decide whether to apply for a franchise which would implicitly involve bidding against sister companies. Furthermore, failure to engage with this process could be see as a lack of faith in their work or even a lack of a will to survive. Many feared that such an approach would be seen by their Local Authority as a dereliction of responsibility. Some companies felt they had no option but to spend the summer of 1999 putting together a franchise bid, whilst others tried to coordinate resistance to the whole concept. The process inevitably bred an atmosphere of suspicion and mistrust.

Whilst there were many in local government and in education who were suspicious of TIE and jealous of any grant aid it received, the fact that Authorities had not been consulted prior to the initial publication of proposals helped ally them to the beleaguered companies. Most companies in Wales were, and are, in receipt of 'partnership funding'. The independent action of ACW was seen by some Local Authorities as ignoring this principal of partnership. Furthermore, should a county-based company lose its ACW funding and cease to exist, was ACW presuming that the traditional Local Authority financial support would, or could, be transferred to a company of the Arts Council's choosing? This, along with very vocal public support in Powys and Gwent [whose companies were to be excluded by the franchises] made reconsideration by ACW inevitable.

As might be expected, the responses from companies varied from the mute to the thunderous depending upon whether they hoped to benefit from the emerging policy or whether their future was endangered. *Gwent Theatre* and *Theatr Powys* launched vigorous campaigns and were supported in this by their Local Authorities. The opposition was based upon a variety of arguments each of which drew support from different sources. The Local Authorities were particularly annoyed by the lack of consultation about the future of 'their' companies. Schools were concerned at the potential reduction and dislocation of the service from their needs. The companies stressed their educational and artistic value and some, notably *Theatr Powys*, saw the plan as an attempt, already begun with ERA and LMS, to marginalize TIE as a force in education and to reduce it to 'educational theatre'. *Theatr Powys* criticized the narrowness of the ACW's consultation process pointing out that it had even overlooked the involvement of the National Assembly government.[17] Like other companies, *Theatr Powys* expressed its concern at the tardiness or inadequacy of ACW guidance and the apparent lack of a clear vision within its policies. There was even the accusation that questions were responded to with obfuscating or inaccurate information. In doing this, *Theatr Powys* had the full support of its Management Board including the Local Authority members. *Theatr Powys* also pointed out that there seemed to be no evidenced link between the sparse responses to the consultation received and the outcomes of the review – the suggested franchising. There was a distinct feeling throughout Wales that a way forward had been decided and that evidence was selected from an impoverished review procedure to justify this pre-conceived policy.[18] The *Theatr Powys* document, together with further closely argued documents from *Gwent Theatre* and others, put enormous pressure on ACW and exposed the frailty of the process and outcomes of the *Drama Strategy*.

Equity, the actors union, also gave their support to the campaign to oppose the Strategy and came to the defence of TIE companies. ACW may have hoped that the plans for developments in the provision of a 'National Theatre' and the setting up of mainstream theatre companies in north and south Wales would have muted Equity's concerns. However, in February 1999, Equity issued a determined criticism of the *Strategy*, stating that 'the idea that this work [TIE] is past its best or is old fashioned and out of touch is ridiculous and does not bear any critical scrutiny.'[19] ACW had succeeded in uniting politicians, Local Authority funders, companies and the acting profession against the proposed review.

To ameliorate the severe levels of criticism that it was suffering, ACW embarked on a much more rigorous consultation process that led to the publication in 2001 of a four hundred page "Audit of Theatre in Education and Theatre for Young People in Wales".[20] This enquiry took evidence from the companies, schools and other interested parties in the presence of both ACW and National Assembly representatives. The resulting report also drew comparisons with YPT arrangements in Europe and Scandinavia. The report evidences the tremendous variety of work going on in Wales and the wide divergences in understanding of the term TIE. The politicians of the increasingly influential National Assembly took a close interest in the process and responded to the outcomes of the consultation by working with ACW to provide additional funding for YPT. There was clearly an attempt to respond to the perceived needs of public and educationalists, and to develop policies that differentiated Wales' priorities from those of England.

As a result, following the 'Audit', ACW launched a completely new policy regarding TIE and YTP in May 2002.[21] Citing the opportunities presented by new monies from the National Assembly, the new proposals referred to expansion, increased training and improved working conditions for arts workers.[22] The publication blames previous problems on lack of investment that lead to the stifling of innovation and development. These problems having been overcome, a truly fundamental change from the 1999 *Strategy* was now possible. Despite having tried to justify its earlier reductive policy in artistic and educational terms, ACW now had the aspiration that 'every child in Wales [was] to experience theatre in education at each of the four Key Stages of the Curriculum. This provision to be free across Wales in both English and Welsh.'[23] Further [and this was a crucial change from previous policy] the ACW favoured 'local delivery by companies rooted in that locality.'[24] Essentially the battle had been won.

On 8th December 2002 a press release from the Welsh Assembly was able to announce an allocation of £1.2 million for TIE with the 'target of providing every child in Wales with theatre in education experience at each of the four stages of the Curriculum.'[25] It is perhaps a measure of the public interest that, in this press release dealing with a number of arts initiatives, the headline concerned TIE. A year later Geraint Talfan Davies, chairman of the Arts Council of Wales, was able to boast [ironically in a speech that centred on the need for a major production company in Wales] that more than 40 per cent of ACW's investment in theatre was in YPT.[26] There are currently still eight companies in Wales and they have recently enjoyed the benefits of 'development' monies.

This small journey through Wales' recent TIE history demonstrates several of the threats that are affecting TIE companies throughout Britain and beyond. There is often a lack of understanding of what TIE *is* and how it works. This misapprehension is not confined to those outside education, but even to teachers, especially those trained since 1990. There is a frequent assumption made that the value of TIE is in the theatrical experience rather than the educational. As a result, companies often feel decisions are being made by those with little respect for or comprehension of the genre. In an era of 'value for money' there is a constant pressure towards short performance pieces playing to large audiences. Participatory programmes, in terms of numbers of children 'served', can appear uneconomic. Given the change of heart by ACW it may seem that this argument had been won and that participatory TIE had been saved; the new strategy not only supported the eight companies but also promised increased levels of funding. However, the trauma of the period 1998–2002 left a legacy of mutual distrust amongst the companies that is only now beginning to dissipate. Moreover, as the study of the work of the companies outlined in the next chapter will reveal, the augmentation of participatory work has not been enhanced. There have always been some marked differences between the development of TIE in England and Wales. In analysing the efficacy of TIE in Wales in 2004, it will be necessary to identify whether the definitions of TIE already offered give an adequate baseline of theory and objectives against which to measure the current praxis. The development of TIE in Wales has been complicated by the issue of language and culture which have always affected the theoretical development.

During the 1970s and 1980s when much English TIE was being inspired by the work of Heathcote and Bolton, there was often a marked reluctance to accept or adopt these ideas, seen as coming from an English tradition. This led to a 'lack of sound theoretical framework and educational theory'[27] though the goal that *theatr mewn addysg*[28] should find its own roots in order to develop with relevance a service to offer the communities of Wales was commendable. Instead, Welsh speaking companies preferred to look over the head of their neighbouring giant to draw influence from international sources. Since Britain was leading the development of this new educational/theatrical hybrid, the influences sourced tended to be theatrically rather than educationally grounded. In this way, much Welsh TIE has perhaps always tended to orientate towards performance projects. However, the centrality of participation has been noted by Welsh commentators. Savill's definition, that 'TIE aims to enable children to learn through experience which is stimulated and motivated by theatre',[29] is augmented by the comment that 'the audience will be assigned a specific role which enables them to react and interact without the burden of self-consciousness.'[30] Further, she talks of the audience being empowered with 'the need to find its own solutions' and to 'reach for a change in understanding.'[31] It is thus argued that definitions of TIE are much the same in Wales as England, though that is not to deny the cultural, educational and theatrical distinctions that may be present. Anne-Marie Taylor's work *Staging Wales* offers one of the few studies of Welsh TIE. She referred to:

> The artistic (and also political) desire to create a specifically Welsh theatrical language, that would by-pass the English mainstream and establish kinship with culturally overshadowed countries.[32]

Gill Ogden feels that TIE in Wales was established 'from England by a process of cultural colonization but which then evolved and adapted to fulfil specific cultural requirements peculiar to the Welsh context.'[33] The terms of this peculiar context will be returned to later. Ogden further notes that the early Welsh companies, as in England, were planning and consulting with teachers but in Wales the distinctive features of the emerging praxis of TIE were missing and did not appear in Wales until English professionals started to join the companies.[34] Savill notes [in 1988] that English language companies 'have begun to use more specific and relevant contexts which have grown out of a better understanding of the Welsh situation.'[35]

This Welsh situation has certain elements that are shared by some English companies, including rurality and funding vagaries. The crucial difference for Wales is that it has two *official* languages. Whilst some English companies may occasionally make forays into responding to the linguistic needs of minority communities, companies in Wales have a responsibility to provide provision that reflects the fact that its two languages have parity. This means that a company such as *Frân Wen* will operate primarily in Welsh, companies such as *Clwyd* and *Arad Goch* will at times produce work in English or Welsh, and companies such as *Theatr Powys* will produce occasional work in Welsh targeted mainly at second-language Welsh Units within schools. The companies of south Wales [*Gwent, Iolo* and *Spectacle*] currently work together to provide one Welsh medium project each year for their Welsh-language schools. There is an active debate about how the distinctiveness of culture impacts on the nature of TIE work in Wales. Central to this is the language 'issue' but it also involves a wider cultural sphere of argument. The history and heritage of performing arts in Wales differs greatly from that of England. It has been noted above that many feel, with some truth, that Wales does not have a tradition of theatre prior to the twentieth century and it is thus a cultural import. Certainly the history of theatre is very different in Wales and in Welsh. Wales does though have a strong heritage of public performance. At the same time Wales can boast of an approach to education which is more embedded in egalitarian and popular principles with, for example, the acceptance of comprehensive education long before it was introduced by the British government in 1976. The historical, political and religious reasons for this are outside the scope of this study, but it is important to recognize that TIE in Wales, whilst sharing much with that of England, is also *consciously* trying to respond to the separate nature of its culture.

For TIE companies in Wales, the key question is whether this separate environment of culture and language implies that TIE will be (or should be) different from that of England. Ian Yeoman, considering the Welsh language work of *Theatr Powys*, acknowledges the problem thus:

> It would be easy in this part of Wales to develop our TIE work in English and simply translate it. We don't do that. The sources of the methodology are the same, but very few of these, I would argue, have been rooted in Wales.[36]

Yeoman's assertion is that it is possible to frame or re-frame a project in Welsh applying participatory constructs whilst operating within the different linguistic and cultural environment of Welsh-speaking Wales. Other companies in Wales would perhaps argue with this approach, and be suspicious of working with methodologies developed by the 'giant' next door.

Further, the country of Wales is not neatly split into Welsh-speaking and English-speaking communities. Within Wales there are communities whose lives are conducted through the medium of Welsh. There are also areas where the Welsh will be peppered with English vocabulary. As is the case with any bilingual community, the preferred language may be different according to the context within which it is being used. Children may use Welsh in school and a mixture of Welsh and English when at play. The language of the home may differ from that of the workplace. For many areas in mid and south Wales children will often have entered education as English monoglots and will have been exposed to Welsh as a second language upon entering school. This presents companies wishing to work in a participatory manner with a particular challenge:

> [Welsh actors] consistently run up against the problem that the capability of the young people to sustain the work that they want is insufficient. We therefore have an extremely particular problem educationally about designing work which is interesting and in Welsh, but that doesn't leave behind an audience which is struggling with a developing vocabulary.[37]

It seems self-evident that any art form will reflect its cultural environment. It is thus clear that TIE in Wales, in either language, should display a distinctiveness from the TIE of other cultures. However, it is also true that art forms influence and are influenced by each other, and this tendency constitutes a creative impulse. For those Welsh companies protective of their differentiation there has been at times an overt avoidance of English influence whilst being at the same time actively engaged in seeking inspiration from further afield. Whilst acknowledging the importance of practitioners such as Heathcote, it has perhaps been this political-cultural approach which has allowed many companies to eschew Anglo-rooted participatory work.

Ironically, whilst the Drama in Education legacy is less apparent in the current work of many companies in Wales, Ogden notes that the cross-border influence can be detected in other aspects of the way in which they work. She notes several areas that are comparable to English practice, observing, for example, that Welsh TIE is planned to contain a fully integrated learning process and the use of facilitators is a common feature. She also recognizes the importance of devising and company involvement, for 'plays written in isolation are often not successful for TIE'.[38] Specialized vocational training is seen to be 'still non-existent'[39] and, whilst some universities and colleges might challenge that assertion, it remained one of the complaints of the companies and Equity during the *Drama*

Strategy debacle. Savill notes the fact that 'a great many of the actor/teachers in Wales are lacking experience and expertise'.[40] If she is correct then this may be another factor affecting the manner in which TIE has developed in Wales. For O'Toole, TIE workers need the status of both 'actor' and 'teacher' that enables them to be called Actor/Teachers. It is probably the case that few performers in TIE companies, in Wales or further afield, could still fulfil this definition. Even in 1989 the HMI Survey of Welsh TIE notes that actors were often experienced in TIE though few had teaching qualifications.[41]

In 1997, despite the financial and educational effects of ERA, Ogden's comments show that there was much that earlier proponents of TIE would recognize as TIE. She defines TIE as seeking to facilitate a change in understanding and notes the use of traditional methods such as participation, 'structured improvisation'[42] and the use of workshops or separate role-play sessions. Referring to the work of Theatr Powys, which she regards as exemplary, she is drawn to comment that 'one should always over- rather than under-estimate the intellectual and empathetic abilities of one's audience, whatever their age or supposed academic abilities.'[43] In her assessment of the work in 1997 she observes the impact of ideas drawn from Heathcote and Boal.

It can be concluded, therefore, that TIE in Wales shared much in common with English TIE and has faced the same challenges from ERA. Welsh TIE has sought to define itself within its own cultural traditions and eschewed much English DIE in favour of multinational influences, though the educational objectives and methodologies remain largely congruent with commentators insisting upon the importance of 'participation' as a defining attribute of TIE in Wales.

Notes

1. OGDEN, G. in A-M. TAYLOR (ed.), op. cit., p. 58.
2. Ibid., p. 51.
3. SHADE, R. "The March of Progress" in *Planet no. 139,* February/March 2002, Aberystwyth, Planet, 2000.
4. ARTS COUNCIL OF WALES, *Chronology outlining the Theatre for Young People franchise history*, ACW, Cardiff, http://www.theatr-cymru.co.uk/news/new061000c.htm, 2000.
5. Ibid.
6. Ibid.
7. Ibid.
8. Ibid.
9. Ibid.
10. BRITISH THEATRE GUIDE, *Towards the Provision of a National Theatre for Wales: A Federal System,* http://www.britishtheatreguide.info/articles/130200e.htm, 2001, p. 5.
11. Ibid.

12. SHADE, R. op. cit., p. 54.
13. Ibid., p. 54.
14. Ibid., p. 55.
15. Ibid., p. 56.
16. Ibid., p. 56.
17. THEATR POWYS, *ACW Draft Drama Strategy for Wales: Theatr Powys Response, Llandrindod, Theatr Powys*, 1999, p. 1.
18. Ibid., p. 3.
19. EQUITY WALES, *Equity Wales response to the proposed new Drama Strategy*, Equity, Cardiff, http:/www.theatr-cymru.co.uk/news/news260299.htm, 1999, p. 1.
20. ARTS COUNCIL OF WALES, *AUDIT OF Theatre in Education and Theatre for Young people in Wales*, Cardiff, Cardiff Arts Marketing, 2001.
21. ARTS COUNCIL OF WALES, *The Future of Theatre for Young People in Wales*, ACW, Cardiff, 2002.
22. Ibid., p. 3.
23. Ibid., p. 5.
24. Ibid., p. 7.
25. RANDERSON, J. Welsh Assembly Culture Minister, "£1.2m for Welsh TIE", *Press Release*, http://www.britishtheatreguide.info/news/welshtie.htm, 2002.
26. UNIVERSITY OF GLAMORGAN, *Press Release 19th November 2003: Planning theatre's legacy of memory*, University of Glamorgan, Pontypridd, 2003. http://www.glam.ac.uk/news/releases/001364.php, p. 1.
27. WOOSTER, R. "From Oppression to Suppression" in *SCYPT Journal: New Voices 16*, London, SCYPT, 1986, p. 13.
28. *theatr mewn addysg* = theatre in education.
29. SAVILL, C. C. "Theatre-in-Education in Wales" in *Planet, the Welsh Internationalist*, no. 67, Aberystwyth, Planet, 1988, p. 49.
30. Ibid., p. 50.
31. Ibid., p. 52.
32. TAYLOR, A-M. (ed.), op. cit., p. 34.
33. OGDEN, G. in A-M. TAYLOR (ed.), ibid., p. 47.
34. Ibid., p. 48.
35. SAVILL, C. C. op. cit., p. 53.
36. See Appendix Three, p. 146.
37. Ibid.
38. OGDEN, G. in A-M. TAYLOR (ed.), op. cit., p. 51.
39. Ibid., p. 52.
40. SAVILL, C. C. op. cit., p. 53.
41. H. M. I., *A Survey of Theatre in Education in Wales*, Cardiff, Welsh Office, 1989, p. 2.
42. OGDEN, G. in A-M. TAYLOR (ed.), op. cit., p. 52.
43. Ibid., p. 53.

Chapter Six

Current TIE Provision in Wales: The Survival of the Fittest?

Aside from the specific challenges and contexts outlined in the previous chapter, there is a large degree of commonality in the artistic, political, financial and educational environment facing TIE companies working in any context. The experience in Wales offers a microcosm of the pressures under which the genre is attempting to survive. In order to quantify the degree and nature of the evolution of TIE, the productions of every ACW-supported company were observed in the summer of 2004.[1] Following each observation a member of the company [usually the director of the production] was formally interviewed using a standard set of questions. Questions 1–10 aimed to identify the working methodology of the company and the way in which the company relates its work to the needs of its clients; the teachers and pupils. The next five questions were designed to give the interviewees an opportunity to discuss the extent to which characteristic TIE identifiers such as workshops and participation are part of their work. Questions 16–18 allowed the respondents to discuss their recruitment policies and training needs and the following three questions invited comment about the development of TIE in Wales. The final group of questions was designed to allow the interviewees to give an overview of their portfolio of work and the funding which facilitates it. An open final question enabled the respondents to add any further thoughts about the current state of TIE not covered by the previous questions. Three of the interviews were conducted by e-mail correspondence but all others were recorded. Transcriptions of all interviews are included in Appendix Three.

In the previous chapters, the characteristics of TIE have been identified, and it has been shown that there is common agreement that TIE involves the careful planning of an integrated learning process using theatrical form. TIE, as distinct from Children's Theatre, aims to achieve a change in understanding usually facilitated through participation, workshops and/or role play attached to a programme using a central theatrical stimulus. The research was designed to identify whether there has been any significant move away from these defining characteristics. Any redefinition or realignment of methodology would not, however, be attributable to companies falling under the philosophies of new directors, for nearly all the artistic leadership of the eight companies in Wales is entrusted to TIE workers who have spent most of their working lives in the genre. Indeed, for several of them this is one of the crucial issues for the future. Jeremy Turner [*Arad Goch*], not entirely in jest, suggests that there should be a policy of pensioning off the current TIE directors. He points out that most of

those now running TIE in Wales started 'when we were angry young things…
[who] wanted to do something different'[2]. Whilst this can sound like the
observation of someone who has mellowed into complacency, his central point
is highly valid; newcomers can feel excluded 'because companies are so intent
on their own practices and philosophies, people perceive that there's no space
within the scene.' (89) When new talent does arise there is 'a danger that new
ideas get adjusted to fit in with what is perceived… and then the newness of the
ideas is lost.' (89) Kevin Lewis [*Theatr Iolo*] voices similar fears:

> I think there will be a crisis in a few years' time because of the fact that the
> directors are ageing! We need new blood, new directors, especially women. (119)

Tim Baker [*Theatr Clwyd Young People's Theatre*] similarly laments the lack of
new directors coming through the system and points out that nearly all TIE in
Wales is the product of the same eight directors. Since companies now rarely
have sustained cores of performers this certainly implies that TIE method and
approach is in the hands of a very small cohort. The philosophies and agendas
of TIE in Wales are dependent upon the practices being employed by eight
directors. If it is accepted that TIE is a crucial part of young people's education,
then this responsibility is a weighty one. Ian Yeoman [*Theatr Powys*] fears that
as the current generation of TIE directors retire from the movement 'there is a
danger that an entire methodology will go down the Swanee.' (145) He is '*not* at
all confident about an ongoing historical development of theatre in education',
(145) though he also acknowledges that 'there is a real drive to protect work for
young people in Wales'. (145)

The issues raised here are those of training, future development and
sustainability, which will be returned to for further consideration. For the
moment let us dwell upon the fact that most TIE directors in Wales have worked
in the genre for often twenty or thirty years. If there has been a change in the
substance of TIE since ERA then it is these directors who have overseen this
change. Have they led any such changes or have they been coerced into serving
the new post-National Curriculum agenda?

As has been pointed out, it is important not to generalize too definitively
upon the state of TIE in Wales from the evidence of the single programme of
any single company. Different programmes require different approaches and
overall philosophy cannot be defined by reference to one sample. In taking a
broad overview of the projects observed for this study, such caveats must be
borne firmly in mind. The overall impression left by the programmes was of the
high production values that underpinned the work. All the projects viewed were
characterized by ingenious and beautiful designs with very high standards of
production. These varied from the set for *Theatr Powys'* version of *Pow Wow*,
which consisted of a circular mat punctuated by abstract sculptures and
arrangements of what would become props or key thematic images, to the main

house production values and budget extended to *Theatr Clwyd Young People's Theatre*'s adaptation of the *Mabinogion* stories which included a cantilevered giant claw. There were inventive, playful and creative sets which without exception transformed the school halls and offered inspiring environments for both actors and audience.

The qualities of direction and performance were of a similarly high standard with performers offering at times exemplary skills in acting, movement and singing. Productions were challenging in their form using, as TIE has always done, a range of Brechtian and Grotowskian devices and sometimes a flexible relationship between character, role and audience. Virtually all the performers demonstrated a very high level of performance proficiency which will have fulfilled more than adequately the demands of the National Curriculum that children should have access to professional production.

The directors interviewed would welcome these observations, since high performance standards are much valued. For *Arad Goch* 'the emphasis is on "theatre" in "theatre in education" (80). *Frân Wen* cites its increasing use of extant work [as opposed to devised material] as leading to 'an increase in production values' (92) and *Gwent Theatre* acknowledges that many programmes have become 'more performance based… [and] the quality of performance has improved' (101). Of all the responses to this area, *Theatr Iolo* is perhaps the most radical in its performance aspirations. *Theatr Iolo* has ceased to use the term TIE to describe its work:

> We are not actually a Theatre in Education company here. Okay, we might say 'yes' to the National Assembly, but we're not there to try and help their social inclusion agenda. We're a theatre company. Our purpose is to create theatre. (114)

For this company the performer has primacy within the company's work:

> You have to follow your own interests and try and create an identity for yourself as a company. (112)

Whereas in the past they felt obliged to say 'yes' to everything, the approach of the company is now that 'we don't have to say "yes" to everything. Let's do what we want' (112). *Spectacle Theatre* demonstrates a similar shift towards the primacy of performance. Steve Davies remarks that the company aims to 'introduce young people to theatre and particularly the fun of theatre' (124). This emphasis is almost universal. Tim Baker [*Theatr Clwyd Young People's Theatre*] feels that 'it is important for children to experience… something of theatrical technique that goes towards making stories.' (129) He is unrepentant about his company's predilection to use Theatr Clwyd as a venue and to bring the audiences to them; 'the building stands for the values of performance – otherwise why build theatres?" (132) Paramount for *Theatr Clwyd Young People's Theatre* is 'the need for very high production values…'. (132)

Given this emphasis on production and performance it is appropriate to consider whether the companies themselves perceive a distinction between TIE and Children's Theatre [CT]. Arguably this was not an issue for TIE companies of the 1970s and early 1980s. For them the hybridization of theatre and drama method in an educational context marked it out clearly from Theatre for Children. It is clear that, for some, this demarcation is no longer acceptable. *Frân Wen* appears to adhere to the traditional view, stating that TIE is 'based on an educational experience rather than entertainment.' (91) *Na n'Og* identifies the key difference as being the level of educational support underpinning the performance and they note that schools book them as much for 'the live theatre experience' (122) as for the educational content of programmes. *Arad Goch* too feels that TIE must have an educational strand running through it, though for them this does not necessarily mean overt themes and learning outcomes. Jeremy Turner acknowledges that 'some of the purists wouldn't call it TIE… This work is somehow linked to their work in schools.' (85) This approach, where the theatrical values are prioritized and the extraction of educational content is secondary, is also reflected in *Gwent Theatre*'s philosophy. Jain Boon feels that the difference between TIE and CT has 'become muddied over the years' (101). She and Gary Meredith cite examples of pieces of CT, which because they are supported by a teaching pack, are justified by companies as pieces of TIE. For Gwent Theatre the key issue is that the material identifies its aims, and targets a specific age group in its inception and development so that educational aims remain central to the piece. Like *Arad Goch*, however, they now place less emphasis on participatory or workshop elements.

At the other end of the TIE scale is *Theatr Iolo* which, as mentioned above, eschews the TIE label. Kevin Lewis accepts that the work of such companies as *Theatr Powys* is TIE 'in the purest sense' (114) because of the way that that company works with small groups in full-day participatory programmes. For Lewis, companies that perform a show and attach a twenty-minute workshop at the end in which 'nothing much of any depth happens' (114) are also not fulfilling the traditional TIE function. He goes on, however, to defend *Theatr Iolo*'s work in schools as providing an experience that can have 'an intelligence and significance' (114).

For *Spectacle Theatre* and *Theatr Clwyd Young People's Theatre* the need to differentiate TIE and CT has even less value. Steve Davies regards the *Where's Andy?* project that was observed as being both TIE and CT:

> The question is, is it effective in what it sets out to do? If it is, let's not bother with the handle. (127)

Tim Baker regards this question as being either 'a "non-question" or *the* question' (133). He cites a change in his approach that has affected his current praxis:

> I began to realize that what we might have been offering to young people in its best and worst form might have been a stunning educational experience but was doing nothing to address the hunger that I wanted them to have for the medium.

Whilst it is clear that *Theatr Clwyd Young People's Theatre* also uses more recognizably TIE methods in some projects, it is also plain that the company sees its prime role as that of a performance company with a responsibility to build the theatre audiences of tomorrow.

Only *Theatr Powys*, under the direction of Ian Yeoman, makes an impassioned case for the separation of the two genres:

> I have absolutely no time for the argument that there is a blurring between the two. The key differences are clear and have been clear since theatre in education was invented. The fact that people want to obfuscate the key differences is another question, but I don't think there's a practical historical blurring. (142)

The nature of these key differences, for Yeoman, is that specific methodologies are being employed 'consciously alongside the theatre, to involve them interactively and spiritually' (143). For those who seek to justify their work as TIE without such praxis, he has little time; 'either you continue to try to develop that as a practice or you don't.' (143)

As has been indicated, the key defining factors that an observer might expect to discern in a piece of TIE would be the presence of such devices as participation, workshops and/or the use of role play with and by the children. Clearly for some directors of TIE in Wales such definitions are no longer sufficient. Most of them indicate that they will use a variety of workshop techniques as appropriate to the project, whilst others believe that this can be superficial and token. On the limited evidence of observations of a single project by each company, it is clear that a range of approaches and philosophies are at work. *Theatr Powys* is working in the most 'traditional' TIE format with full participation by the children throughout the daylong project. The children's contributions were structured and developed by the actors working as facilitators, as characters and often in a 'twilight' area between character and role. The contributions and interventions of the children were used by the actors in the development of the meanings within the story of the characters. Whilst all the programmes observed, with the exception of *Theatr Iolo*'s production *The Journey*, boasted a workshop of some description, this was the only project to have used a participatory methodology. This approach remains central to the company's work. Through participation children are encouraged to 'create the motivation to do the thing' (141). *Theatr Powys* prides itself on its adherence to 'educational methodologies' (141). In Yeoman's view the paucity of the participatory method in Wales is a result of drawn-out financial pressures, but it could also be argued that participatory and drama praxis were never as strong in TIE in Wales because of the perceived cultural imperialism from English drama theorists referred to in previous chapters.

The only other full-day project was that based on *The Mabinogion* stories by *Theatr Clwyd Young People's Theatre*. In this project about two hundred children attended Theatr Clwyd for the day and, in two groups, either saw a performance in the morning followed by a workshop in the afternoon or vice versa. Thus, the content of the workshop was not dependant upon the play nor was an exploration of the play undertaken through the workshop. Indeed, the pre-workshop was completely different from the post-workshop. The particular workshop observed [the post-workshop] was based on the construction and use of puppets [which had been a feature of the show] and concluded with the children re-enacting parts of the play using their own puppets. There was clearly an educational purpose at work and the children were demonstrating construction and team-working skills, though performance elements were somewhat weak. They had had an educationally and artistically fulfilling day which the teachers had enjoyed and found valuable in a range of ways. Within its own terms the project was undoubtedly a success. However, the 'Mabinogion' consist of archetypal stories and contain elements which could have also inspired a very different educational approach. Amongst the possible themes present in the play were child abuse, post-natal depression, revenge, honesty, trust, the justification of violence in self-defence, faithfulness, duty, child abduction, justice, rules, expectations, forgiveness, the death penalty and breaking taboos. Whilst it is unfair to criticize a project for not doing that which it did not set out to do, and whilst accepting that such issues could not be dealt with effectively with a group of a hundred children, it is permissible to consider whether a TIE programme should regard the investigation of such material as its natural territory. For Baker there are few set rules about the employment of workshop techniques. *Theatr Clwyd Young People's Theatre* still occasionally uses what the director refers to as a 'traditional workshop at the end of the play' (132). The workshops for *The Mabinogion* were actually led by freelance drama workers following the template set down by the Education Officer and in this way the process of workshop and theatre stimulus have been completely separated. Baker regards these workshops as having huge value to teachers. For him there are no fixed rules. He does believe that participation is an essential element of TIE but he does not accept that, within his definition, that the young people attending *The Mabinogion* were *not* participating. Clearly there are issues here of definition and semantics, for if all audiences are 'participants' does that imply that there is no difference between participatory TIE and performance-centred CT?

All the other projects observed were of a much shorter duration: typically a performance piece of about forty-five minutes with elements of workshop or discussion before and/or after. *Arad Goch* offered the most recognizable TIE/drama package. There was a short pre-performance session in the classroom in which the characters and themes were introduced and the children 'contracted' into an acceptance of the convention that the same actors would be playing different characters. Following the play, the children were involved in a drama workshop in which they undertook occupational mime, slow-motion games, were encouraged to develop skills of cooperation, and learnt one of the songs from the play. This linked to a major theme within the play concerning negotiation within friendship. The workshop was highly structured and the seventy participants were led through a series of activities which enabled them to show that they had received the messages of the play. The nature of the work was reminiscent of Slade and Way and the children were not asked to investigate deeply the nature of rivalry and personal ambition within the context of family and friend relationships. Once again, with such numbers in the small hall and only twenty minutes at the company's disposal, it would have been difficult to organize a workshop in any other way. The question arising is whether *Arad Goch* would have *preferred* to have worked in more depth over a longer period of time; whether it is a matter of educational philosophy, or economics and logistics that defines the nature of their workshop approaches. For Turner the structure of their TIE programmes is founded on a long-standing decision to separate performance and workshop or 'practical discussion' (83). The company prefers to work in this way rather than with 'traditional' TIE method. Further, he states that 'I don't think there is any more such a thing as traditional TIE. I'm not sure that there ever was. There was a way of working that some companies used. But I don't think that is the only TIE pattern' (83).

Gwent Theatre's programme *Home Front* had even less participation with little workshop involvement. Following the play, the children were allowed ten minutes to interview the stage manager about the play whilst the rest of the company undertook the strike. The questions put to the children were about 'what the characters were like' and 'how they changed'. The children were then invited to ask questions and these centred around technical and performance aspects of the show. There was no opportunity for the children to reflect upon the behaviour or the characters, nor to investigate the feelings [and thus their own responses] through, for example, depiction work or Forum Theatre. This is offered as an observation, not a criticism, since it was clear that the company was working on a very tight schedule. Again the issue is whether this is the preferred way of working, a way of working enforced by practicalities, or even a way of working that is dictated by the training and experience of the actors. In the interview Jain Boon maintains that decisions about workshops are based on the needs of the material and the time available. For this particular project *Gwent Theatre* feels that the material could have been developed to be a full-day participatory programme, but that the decision was taken to create a performance piece supported by teacher resources. One of the reasons cited for this decision was that 'schools have become more reluctant to put aside a whole day' (98). Another reason is the cost and the demand to cover more schools more often. Meredith misses 'very much not being able to do the full-day programme, but I don't think it necessary that every programme is a full-day programme. I've never thought that, even in the "good ol' days"' (98).

A similar approach was taken by *Theatr Na n'Og* in *Big Bad Wolf*. At the end of the performance the actors led a discussion that encouraged the children to talk about their favourite part of the play and then went on to ask questions of the audience which tested their recall of the story. Again, educational value is present in terms of oracy, but the deeper themes of friendship and trust were less explored. Rachel Clancy [Education Officer] explains that for this project, as with most of their Key Stage One work, it was only considered necessary to have a brief discussion. When working on a set text for Key Stage Four they are more likely to include a workshop. For *Theatr Na n'Og* 'it depends upon the needs of the show… [and] as with this show, there is often audience involvement' (121).

Spectacle Theatre's performance of *Where's Andy?* was sandwiched between two short discussion sessions in the classroom which were designed to break the ice and to introduce the themes and then, following the show, to gauge whether the children were able to relate the issues of the performance to their own lives. The aim was to help the children 'individually and collectively make sense of the experience' (126). As part of this 'traditional' TIE, questioning techniques are employed, turning 'the questions back to the audience for them to answer for themselves'. (126) Davies explains that, as with most of the interviewees, the approach to workshop technique is flexible. Dependent upon the needs of the project, workshops can last ten minutes or half a day. The function of a workshop remains the same for *Spectacle Theatre*: 'meaning is made by the audience and we are interested in the meaning they make from it. We do not tour "messages"…'. (127) This approach is very similar to that taken by *Frân Wen* and, like *Where's Andy?*, *Lleisiau Yn Y Parc* was based on a storybook which the children were able to reference as part of the follow-up activities in school. In the pre-show session the storybook was introduced and the children were encouraged and 'contracted' to watch the play with 'magic spectacles'. Following the play the themes of the performance [friendship, trust, 'safe-play'] were discussed and finally the children were invited to remove their magic spectacles. In her response to the questionnaire, Iola Ynyr, *Frân Wen*'s director, states that the utilization of a workshop will depend upon various factors. She maintains that 'it might be the case that a workshop is unsuitable for a certain age group' (91). There is an apparent implication here that drama technique is less valid with young children – a claim which many drama theorists and teachers would perhaps dispute. Another limitation cited is the pressure of numbers that have to be accommodated in a performance. She feels that the work pack provided 'is sufficient to initiate discussion and address issues' (91).

Of all the companies observed, only *Theatr Iolo* offered no workshop element as part of their project. The reasons for this are partly, Lewis suggests, related to the fact that actors do not tend to have the skills and that short-term contracts prevent such skills being acquired. However, he too cites the financial pressures that have led to *Theatr Iolo* becoming a more performance-orientated company playing to large audiences. For those companies that have to charge schools this is clearly an issue; a project can be made viable only if the costs are defrayed over a large number of pupils. Beyond these practical issues there are more methodological and policy considerations at work. Lewis reports that 'at some point I just got fed up with struggling with workshops and started to think "I just want to start concentrating on the play"' (113). As the pressures to accept larger audiences grew he found the notion of the workshop becoming meaningless. He is now more interested in workshopping with young people prior to a project as a means to create material for a play, rather than as a way of analysing the content afterwards.

Since participatory and workshop techniques employed within TIE projects are predicated upon knowledge of drama methodologies, all TIE directors in Wales were questioned about their influences in this area. Later it will be noted that few TIE performers now have a background in teaching, and few drama or acting courses deal with TIE in any depth. It is therefore in the skills and training of the directors of companies that such drama method is likely to reside. Turner notes that the ideas of people such as Heathcote 'are there – they've always been there', but such ideas are rarely referred to 'as a matter of policy' (84). Similarly Baker admits an admiration for Heathcote and also to Boal, but theatrical approaches are much more central for *Theatr Clwyd Young People's Theatre*. *Frân Wen* has also in the past received training in Heathcote's approaches but their reference to her work is couched in terms of admiration 'for her unpatronising approach towards children' (91) rather than in a live praxis in regular use. *Gwent Theatre* also cites Heathcote and Bolton, though for the younger members of the team their knowledge is second-hand, derived through such practitioners as Louise Osborn. The company feels that ideas get handed down and adapted to suit contemporary needs. Meredith notes that 'sometimes you think you have invented something yourself, but it is usually out there somewhere' (100). Even the highly performance-orientated

Theatr Iolo acknowledges the work of Heathcote, though Lewis feels that 'I don't know so much about that stuff now' (114). *Na n'Og* cites no drama theorists, their drama influences coming through listening 'to what children and teachers are saying about the work' (122). Clancy prefers to 'devise my own way to create participatory work' (122). Steve Davies, with a long history of TIE work in Wales, refers only to the participatory work of Leeds TIE Company as a drama influence. For *Theatr Powys*, the only company regularly undertaking participatory work, Heathcote and Bolton are again acknowledged, as is the development and contexualization of these ideas through such practitioners as Geoff Gillham, Tag MacEntegert and David Davis.

Many companies were more fulsome when it came to identifying theatrical influences, especially international ones. *Theatr Iolo* clearly identifies itself within a European context and takes much theatrical impulse from its links with companies and festivals across the continent. *Arad Goch* has had an even longer tradition of looking beyond the English giant next door to the theatrical inspiration offered by Europe and Scandinavia. *Gwent Theatre* cites the work of neighbouring *Theatr Powys*, but also companies such as *Shared Experience* and their treatment and exploration of German Expressionism. Influences upon *Na n'Og*'s Geinor Jones include the *Laramie Project* and 'the energy and bravado' of the National Theatre's *Guys and Dolls*. Stylistically she has also been influenced by *Theatre de Complicité*. Davies at *Spectacle Theatre* cites David Mamet, Kantor and the Theatre of the Dead.

Frân Wen does not note any particular dramaturge or cultural influence, mentioning only that 'each project has its own theatrical style' (91). Similarly, Baker, at *Theatr Clwyd Young People's Theatre*, feels that he draws from an unspecified range of influences that reflect 'very high production values and simplicity of storytelling' (132). Yeoman also admires European work that involves stillness and depiction. He feels that too much of the work of some other companies is influenced by television drama.

The responses to the questions about drama and theatre influences are reflected in the work of the companies. Production values and styles clearly owe a great deal to international influence, and Wales should be proud of the eclectic variety and creativity of the output of its companies. It may be argued, though, that there is a certain paucity in the adoption and adaptation of sound *drama* theory that is leading to an underachievement in the *exploration* of this strong performance work. Some directors will argue that the work must speak for itself, with the help of teaching materials, and others will point to the pressures to cover huge catchments with limited resources. Whatever the reasons, it does seem clear that the use of drama-derived methodologies as part of TIE are under pressure from both companies' policies and the demands of the education system.

One of the key educational 'givens' with which teachers, pupils and, thus, TIE companies have to deal, is the National Curriculum. One of the questions put to directors concerned the extent to which the demands of the Curriculum guided the content or form of their work. In general terms, and in accordance with the pre-eminence given to production values over educational content, many companies felt that they were not enslaved to the demands of the Curriculum. It was generally agreed that the educational content is within the programmes ready to be mined and extracted by the teacher, but rarely were Learning Objectives identified, even when a teaching pack was supplied as part of the project. Turner sums up the situation thus:

> It is only after we've had the initial idea that we turn to the Curriculum to see where we could use the Curriculum as a 'coat hanger' (83).

Theatr Iolo employs an Education Liaison Officer and issues, often highly original, teaching materials. However, they avoid actually pointing out the Curriculum links from their work because, as Lewis puts it, 'actually they [the teachers] know all that' (111). Similarly, *Theatr Powys* feels that its specific knowledge of the National Curriculum may not be up to date, though Learning Objectives such as 'oral expression, communication, self-discipline, sociability, other cultures' (141) would be covered by most TIE work. Yeoman points out though, that 'at no point did we sit down and diagnose what the needs of Key Stage One [were]' (141).

Frân Wen take a more structured approach with its work packs 'based on the curricular objectives of the specific age group' (90). They also reference the Curriculum and give examples of possibilities for cross-curricula activities. *Gwent Theatre* is also starting to adopt this approach. Meredith feels that in the past relation to Curriculum work was 'quite vague, but we are now much keener to be able to identify the links' (97). This is becoming necessary, he feels, to assist teachers in justifying the time spent on a TIE project, especially at secondary school level. He also recognizes the dangers inherent in this; that the company could become 'a sort of "menu service" for the National Curriculum' (97). Basically, he feels the links are there in any piece of work and *Gwent Theatre* sees its task to help teachers by pointing these links out. In an appeal that TIE practitioners since the 1960s would recognize, Meredith asks that the company and its work should not be seen as 'the creatures that belong to the English or the Drama departments' (98). *Na n'Og* already has a policy of charting the Curriculum links in its support material:

> It is clearly indicated where there are links to Learning Objectives, Tasks, Key Skills and what resources are needed. We think this is very important for teachers. For them everything needs to be justified in terms of the Curriculum. (121)

The company does not, however, find this limiting artistically, believing that 'there is plenty of scope to be creative whilst giving the schools what they need...' (121).

Whatever the state of TIE in Wales in 2004, the drama and theatre heritages are by definition intrinsic. Issues of personality, character, motivation and relationships, will always be present. As has been indicated, the art of theatre and theatre in education are predicated upon a human being's ability to objectify his or her experience and to learn through that experience. This can be a subjective or an objective process, and in 'traditional' TIE usually involved a combination of the two. If drama methodology is on the wane in TIE and theatre experience is pre-eminent, this does not detract from the value that any piece of theatre may offer to an understanding of the human condition with all its contradictions and confusions. For this reason many companies particularly cite the value of their work in respect of the PSHE curriculum where a consideration of attitudes, beliefs, relationships and personal pressures are demanded. This is especially noted by Davies at *Spectacle Theatre* and Jones at *Na n'Og*. *Arad Goch* also remarks that the themes of *O Fore Gwyn Tan Nos* have clear resonance within the PSHE curriculum. Meredith makes the same point as regards *Home Front* and, whilst *Theatr Iolo* does not make the claim for *The Journey*, the key theme of 'co-operation' clearly fulfils the same Curriculum need. Baker, referring to *The Mabinogion* points out that the work has reference to the Curriculum demand for a knowledge of Welsh culture but he does not refer to the potential PSHE content of the work.

There was a time when TIE companies, eager to prove their educational and academic credentials, were renowned for producing weighty, worthy and voluminous teaching packs. In the summer of 2004 all companies except *Theatr Powys* produced a pack to accompany their work. *Theatr Powys* sometimes produces packs and sometimes does not. They are very proud of some of their past materials, produced by the director and actors, but feel that occasionally the time devoted to them can be wasted since often the material may not be employed by the over-burdened teacher. In such cases, the participatory nature of the work is seen to provide a supremely valid way of investigating issues within the sole context of the programme itself. At *Arad Goch*, the materials will usually be produced by the director and there has been a move away from the heavily researched material towards packs 'which have more readily usable ideas and tasks...' (83). The worksheets in the pack for *O Fore Gwyn Tan Nos* included ideas for vocabulary development, creative and letter writing, music, art and numeracy. There are suggestions for discussion work but no specifically drama ideas.

Frân Wen's pack details the Curriculum links in accordance with their policy of Curriculum relevance. Packs also contain activities, poetry and 'other relevant literature' (90). Rachel Clancy, at *Na n'Og*, coordinates teaching materials for every show in her role as Education Officer, working closely with teachers to decide the content. The policy at *Spectacle Theatre* is to provide resources and suggestions for teachers for every project and in the case of *Where's Andy?* this also included a copy of the cartoon book that inspired the play. Davies hopes that this actually took the TIE experience back into the home, as the child would be likely to discuss the play and the book with his or her parents. *Theatr Clwyd Young People's Theatre* TIE uses the offices of their permanent Education Officer to both produce resource materials and suggestions for class work and also to undertake visits to schools to run workshops.

Gwent Theatre has taken the step of 'sub-contracting' the teacher's materials to its teachers advisory panel. This has the two-fold advantage of relieving the company of the burden and also ensuring that the packs contain such information as a teacher might usefully need and be likely to use. It also has the positive effect of necessitating close liaison between company and teachers panel during the devising/rehearsal process. However, even this company reports that use of the material by teachers is 'patchy' (97). They feel that the more closely related is the material to the National Curriculum the better used it is. The pack for *Home Front* contains much background historical information, including photographs, as well as a description of the genesis of the project from the points of view of each of the production team. Tasks include suggestions for oracy work, design work and discussion topics. Clearly there is an attempt here to respond to the Curriculum demands for an appreciation of theatre, as well as offering support to the wider literacy Learning Objectives and discussion of the themes of the play.

Theatr Iolo are trying to develop novel forms of teaching materials and refer to occasions when they have included a reproduction of the Picasso painting which inspired the play, and on another occasion, a teapot containing items and stimuli relating to the performance piece. When a traditional pack is produced they try to keep it succinct, as 'there is so much resource material around for teachers that you don't want to overburden them' (111). The pack for *The Journey* takes a more generic approach than others viewed, containing information about the music used in the production and stimuli for work on storytelling and art activities. There are also tasks that require the children to recall the events of the play and the motives of the characters, essentially as a way to get the children to talk about feelings and relationships. In fact, the themes of friendship, negotiation, relationships and behaviour were common to many of the programmes on tour in 2004. It is tempting to consider whether companies are finding this PSHE – related material 'safer' than former TIE subject material that might often touch on social issues with more contentious undertones. Here again, though, we arguably now live in a 'less political' age where issues of class, challenge to authority and personal morality are less a matter of debate, having been subsumed in an accepted 'third way' apoliticism. TIE may be responding to genuine contemporary needs.

The questions regarding training and recruitment[3] elicited responses that demonstrated, often passionate, opinions. Indeed, several directors took the opportunity to muse further on the need for TIE in Wales to develop skills for the future of the genre. Clearly it is felt that this is a key issue for the survival and development of TIE and an attempt will now be made to summarize the contribution that training, or the lack of it, may be making to the current state of TIE in Wales.

The term 'actor/teacher', once the defining designation of a performer in TIE, has by many been rejected. In the early days of TIE, company members were as likely to have come from the educational as the theatre world. Many companies, especially those employing 'actor/teachers' on LEA contracts, would positively seek out those with both theatrical experience and a teaching qualification. This was already breaking down before ERA, as companies moved, under financial pressure, to short-term Equity contracts. In 2004 there is no company in Wales that demands teacher training of its performers, though many recognize it as an advantage since, in Turner's words, 'they can speak the same jargon as the teachers' (86). Many stress that high-level performance skills are the sole criterion. Amongst these are *Arad Goch*, *Gwent Theatre*, *Spectacle Theatre* and *Theatr Clwyd Young People's Theatre*. *Theatr Powys*, which arguably uses a great deal of teaching skill in its participatory approach, similarly does not prioritize teaching skills in its employment policy. Yeoman feels that, as current teachers have come through the post-ERA teacher training system, their skills would, in any case, be less appropriate:

> A lot of new teachers have been taught the kind of educational theory that applies to the late 1980s and 90s... A lot of classroom teachers don't know very much about the kind of educational approach we take. So being a classroom teacher does not qualify you and being an actor does not qualify you... I always look for people with a sense of drama and theatre that are interested in young people...(144)

Frân Wen asks neither for teacher training nor experience in TIE, though the company tends to use actors who have worked in the field previously. *Theatr Iolo*'s experience is that those actors who are teacher trained tend to be weaker performers and it feels that by employing an Education Officer the previous symbiosis of 'theatre' and 'education' has been advantageously separated. Similarly at *Na n'Og*, the only company member teacher trained is the Education Officer, but to have these skills in the performance team is thought to be 'not really necessary' (122) though a candidate's possession of workshop skills would be an advantage.

Thus, somewhat ironically, as the educational system has become channelled by structures and strictures, TIE has distanced itself from close involvement with teaching criteria. Instead it has either, like *Theatr Powys*, clung on to a previous pedagogical framework of child-centred learning, or, like most of the other companies in Wales, focussed on theatre performance from which educationalists [based in the company or the schools] can draw out the teaching context. Upon the evidence of the eight programmes observed, it is clear that the teaching skills demanded of performers have been reduced when compared to early TIE. However, Yeoman's assertion, that performers in TIE are more than 'just' actors and that they need to have an interest and drive to work with young people, would be accepted by most of the companies in Wales. Baker defines the issue similarly. He asserts the primacy of performance skill, but requires of his actors that 'they are hungry for being more than just actors'. He wants them to be 'hungry to be facilitators and also devisors' (134). Like other directors in Wales he finds that young actors have to learn to move beyond an 'actor-centred' approach in order to become useful performers in the company's work.

It therefore follows that those entering the TIE profession require skills beyond those that a qualified actor might possess. Many companies in Wales perceive a 'training gap' in the skills that are offered to new actors. Training in drama teaching is far less prevalent than it was in the 1960s and 1970s and, in any case, teachers with drama training are now less likely to find a place within a TIE company. The companies of Wales, emphasizing the performance skills that are required for their work, seem to be looking to drama schools to make up this deficit. Turner maintains that 'there is not one course in Wales which adequately trains actors to work in TIE' (88). He is disparaging of isolated modules that claim to teach TIE method in a 'seven-week module' (88). He further believes that 'to teach kids what TIE is, that is exactly the wrong way to do it... they need the expertise of the professional to know what TIE is. It is such a delicate and sensitive area' (88). *Gwent Theatre*'s solution to the problem is to try to get back to the notion of a core company, where methodology and skill can be developed within the team. Many of the directors interviewed note that the rehearsal period involves a time-consuming amount of induction and training when working with performers new to TIE, though, those skills, according to Meredith, 'can be learned' (102). Davies, at *Spectacle Theatre*, reports that '[it is] very difficult to recruit any actor with any training in TIE unless they have experience from other companies' (127). He believes that training is a key issue for the future of TIE in Wales. This analysis is shared by Yeoman who feels that 'training institutions are not training people to do [TIE] anymore' (144). He seeks to build, re-forge and protect 'that theoretical and practical approach to the work' (144). He further feels that the infrastructure of training still does not recognize the value of the work and that, as a result, 'the research, training and development in TIE is actually happening on the ground' (145). If he is correct then the outlook for TIE is not positive, for if no analysis or development is taking place in academic and training institutions, then the future of TIE lies in the hands of a small band of ageing TIE theorist/directors. Whilst the skills may be passed down to a new generation of actors, the pedagogical analysis that underpins and frames the approach may not. There is a danger perhaps of allowing TIE to become a 'folk art' where the rituals of structure are followed but no longer with the pedagogical passion or understanding that inspired the original protagonists.

Despite this training deficit, most companies feel comparatively secure following the new ACW TIE/YPT policy that followed the *Drama Strategy* debacle. No doubt there will be twists and turns to this story as local authorities attempt to deal with financial crises or the ACW finds its policies under the scrutiny, or even the control, of political 'short-termism'. Turner acerbically points out that whilst politicians talk about TIE as the jewel in the Welsh crown 'they don't actually polish it too often' (87). However, assuming that the financial future is comparatively uneventful and that funding inequalities between companies can be ameliorated through cooperation between central and local government, what is the current state of TIE in Wales as a genre and what future is perceived? This is a fundamental question concerning the evolution of TIE.

At the heart of any debate about the quintessential descriptors of theatre in education is the perceived place of the needs of the child within the praxis. It has been shown how notions of using theatre and drama to educate evolved from beliefs in child-centred learning and a wish to identify and serve children's needs. One of the questions put to the directors early in the interview concerned the extent to which 'the needs of children' influenced the development or content of programmes; a question suggested by Chris Cooper of *Big Brum*. The responses to this question are revealing.

Arad Goch feel they achieve this through personal experience and the creation of an informal group of young people who they may turn to for reaction and response. *Gwent Theatre* makes conscious attempts to look beyond the Curriculum to respond to 'what we think is important for children' (95). Rachel Clancy, for *Na n'Og*, cites the theme of 'playing' in *Big Bad Wolf* as an example of how children's needs are responded to; 'the needs of the children are always there' (120). *Spectacle Theatre* too believe that the needs of children are 'key to the company's work', believing in the 'beneficial experience of theatre [in] allowing us to risk-take in a safe environment' (125). Baker, at *Theatr Clwyd Young People's Theatre*, recognizes that the children are the ultimate recipients of the work although there is a necessity to work through the teachers initially. He gives the example of a World War Two project that had been marketed as such to teachers even though the ultimate concern of the company was the issue of 'families under stress' and thus aimed at the young people. The company has a policy of sending actors into schools at the beginning of a project 'to try and get a little bit into their world' (131). *Theatr Powys* is passionate about the importance of responding to young people's needs and feels it is something they address '*all the time*' (139). For Yeoman, the key function of TIE is to be able 'to humanize the way in which young people communicate with each other.' (139) Other companies display a different approach. *Frân Wen* feels that it is able to gauge the needs of children through questionnaires with teachers. *Theatr Iolo* goes even further, reporting that no attempt is made to identify the needs of children and that it is no longer a question that needs to be addressed; it is sufficient that children 'should be exposed to really good material' (109). Most companies in Wales thus feel that they are responding to the needs of children and, in theory, these are prioritized above the needs of teachers and the National Curriculum. Is the education that takes place through TIE, therefore, as it always was; child-centred and progressive, offering a safe context for reflection and emotional growth? These interpretations of the notion of responding to the needs of children are perhaps the key to determining whether TIE has continued to evolve using the precepts of the early pioneers, or whether contemporary TIE has become mutated. TIE was a hybrid built upon the rootstock of drama and theatre. It will now be considered whether one of the genetic parents has begun to dominate or whether the hybrid continues to thrive.

Notes

1. See Appendix One.
2. See Appendix Three, 88. The full context of all quotations can be found by referencing the appropriate interview in Appendix Three.
3. See Appendix Four, Summary Table II.

Chapter Seven

Conclusion: Evolution or Mutation?

From the productions and responses to the subsequent interviews, it is possible to make some broad observations and to draw general conclusions about the current format and philosophy of TIE in Wales. Such conclusions, however, will be in the nature of an evidenced impression, since it would be unreasonable to extrapolate definitively from these individual samples of work.

In earlier chapters it was indicated that the origins of TIE were rooted in post-war theatrical and educational developments. As such, TIE tended to deviate in its form from pre-war repertory and proscenium styles of theatre, and its educational content showed considerable indebtedness to the new progressive approaches to schooling. The theatrical genealogy of Brecht, 'alternative' theatre and from agitprop theatre has been indicated. Additionally, the rise, and subsequent fall, of progressive and child-centred educational policies has been charted, and it has been noted that such ideas found natural champions and resonances in the subject of drama in schools. It has also been argued that TIE, from 1965, sought to create a symbiosis of new theatrical genres, separate from Children's Theatre, with these pedagogical innovations.

The implications of this new 'hybrid' were often profound. The approach to teaching from the 'de-schoolers' and 'progressivists' inevitably caused consternation amongst traditionalists in education and politics. Further, the notion of teaching to facilitate questioning and challenge was an anathema to many on the political right. This caused a suspicion and mistrust that was felt by both DIE and TIE. The potential for conflict was exacerbated by the influence on TIE of Brechtian notions of 'scientific thinking' and a belief in the power and duty of theatre to pursue change. It was only in the particular environment of the liberalizing 1960s that such a hybrid would have found the artistic, educational and financial support that permitted it to flourish.

The specific nature of the education pursued by both DIE and TIE has also been examined. From a range of drama theorists from Finlay-Johnson and Caldwell Cook, to Slade, Way, Heathcote and Bolton came the developing notion that education should be about nurturing the whole child. Children should be encouraged to understand, to empathize, to reflect and to contemplate how the world could and should be. For many teachers and commentators, drama could be used not only to guide and develop the child within the confines of a drama lesson, but could also be the unifying force for the whole curriculum. For DIE, and later for TIE, cross-curriculum approaches enabled the private world of the developing child to engage with the wider education of which he or she was a part.

It has been shown that the basic human quiddity upon which drama, theatre and theatre in education are founded is the ability to play. Leaving aside aspects of play which facilitate the art of acting *per se*, drama and TIE are founded, it has been argued, upon the human being's natural inclination to make sense of the world and the self within the world, through play. Application of this facet of human behaviour is clearly to be observed in the work of the drama theorists mentioned, along with Boal and the developing practice of drama therapists. Whilst 'play' is also clearly evident in Theatre, it is a more central aspect of both Drama and Theatre in Education since the children, *as participants*, are actively involved in the unfolding simulation led by the drama teacher or TIE team. It has been argued that this participatory element, which may take the form of role play or 'frame', was a defining characteristic of the developing genre of TIE from the mid 1960s, using children as critical observers and commentators.

It has also been noted that when the educational climate changed in the wake of the *Black Papers* and Callaghan's speech at Ruskin College in 1976, that TIE came under threat. The twelve years that followed saw the growth of a consensus away from progressive educational ideas towards a more utilitarian approach. This culminated in the Education Reform Act of 1988 which both introduced strict curriculum demands upon schools and, through LMS, initiated potential financial threats to peripatetic school services, including TIE. As a result, in the early 1990s many companies were disbanded despite the fact that the National Curriculum both placed emphasis upon the need for access to theatre for schoolchildren and the encouragement of PSHE work. TIE was well placed to fulfil these demands, but the implications of serving a narrowly defined curriculum proved unpalatable to the political orientation of some companies.

This study has focussed upon the nature of TIE in contemporary Wales, and it has therefore been pointed out that there has often been a distinctiveness to the situation in that country. Perhaps as the result of responding to the particular needs of providing theatre in a rural country, the Arts Council in Wales has always been more disposed to support small-scale touring companies. Thus, in Wales, many companies were able to survive even when local authority funding became less secure. The fortunate situation, fifteen years after ERA, is that every county in Wales has access to the services of a touring educational company. In the previous chapter the results of a survey of these companies has been analysed in an effort to identify whether this survival has been predicated upon a judicious adaptation to the changing environment which has managed to retained the identifying characteristics of TIE. This involves a consideration of the converse possibility: that companies have survived through deserting these basic tenets and become a new genetic strain adapted to survive the changed climate of educational utilitarianism and funding criteria.

TIE has been defined in a variety of ways, usually centring on the use of theatrical and educational techniques and especially the use of participation. For Baskerville 'the key word was participation'.[1] The participants, or percipients, will normally be expected to engage with the drama in ways that

Disgrified in MA [handwritten margin note]

encourage them to observe, feel and respond in a safe context. It is held that this approach allows children to be objective and empathetic at the same moment and to thus learn about themselves and themselves within the world. Itzin thus describes TIE as 'a means whereby children can come to understand and control their environment'.[2]

It is thus argued that TIE essentially involves the children actively, deriving its theory from DIE, whilst theatre which seeks to impart information is better termed 'educational theatre'. It is posited that the unique feature of TIE is that is uses the child's ability to play and offers a safe context for reflection and personal development. It has been TIE's ability to hybridize the worlds of play, reflection, personal development and self-education together with theatrical constructs that gave it its value. If this is now being ignored, then TIE may be regarded as little more than a spectator activity in schools that could be easily replaced by theatre visits or even video, supported by teaching materials. However, we cannot expect that TIE will not change for that would make the genre sterile and unresponsive. Boon points out that 'how we do it might change, but the need for what it can do will always be there'.[3] Without the pedagogic analysis underpinning the work, TIE is in danger of mutating into a completely different creature. Crucially, TIE must respond to the needs of children rather than educators. It is upon this criterion that any judgement must be made. Without the rigour of sound educational theory, the product will become an adjunct to Children's Theatre, and it is notable that already some directors admit to finding it hard to separate the forms.

The current nature of contemporary TIE in Wales having been outlined, it is now possible to determine whether TIE in Wales has been the subject of an evolutionary process or whether it can no longer be regarded to be part of the original genus.

It is clear from the programmes seen, along with the additional evidence of the interview responses, that a discernable change in attitude towards the nature and function of TIE has taken place. Broadly, these changes can be categorized into two key areas. First of these is the blurring of distinctions between TIE and Children's Theatre. In a statement to the Arts Council of Great Britain in 1984, the committee of the SCYPT Journal explained the differences clearly. Children's Theatre's primary aim is to '*entertain* or to *increase the appreciation of theatre as an art form*'. TIE aims to '*use* theatre and drama for educational purposes... to teach about something *other* than theatre or theatre skills.' The editorial also offers a definition of Educational Theatre as being '*educational*, but generally restricted *to a play for a large number of young people.*'[4] From the evidence presented it is clear that the latter most accurately describes current work in Wales. However, as has been shown, several directors challenged the validity of such distinctions. They point to an increased emphasis on 'production values' and the theatrical skills of the teams whilst adhering to educational aims. There were also those, however, who maintained a clear distinction between the genres, and, in one case,[5] this distinction was quite vehemently defended.

The second area of philosophical change is less tangible and raises significant issues for an attempt to make judgements about the pertinence of current TIE in Wales. The changing nature of education in Britain since ERA, outlined in previous chapters, can be broadly characterized as a move from progressive, heuristic and child-centred learning to a more utilitarian and proscriptively tested system within the National Curriculum. Early TIE can be seen as both the product and instigator of 'progressive' educational values, but since these values have ostensibly changed, the question thus arises to what extent the function and approaches of current TIE should also change. Assuming TIE still has a function in schools, should it seek to reflect and augment current educational approaches and philosophies? If the original TIE methodologies are seen as the product of a particular moment in educational, theatrical and social history, then it may well be the case that it is erroneous to expect that TIE today should be pursuing former educational goals. This is the argument for seeing current TIE praxis as the contemporary manifestation of an ongoing evolutionary process. There is a pedagogical-political issue to be confronted if TIE seeks still to provide an educational approach that is no longer deemed appropriate by the state or its educational servants. Now that the pedagogical framework has changed, is it possible, or desirable, for a TIE company to draw upon those theories of education which are predicated upon Rousseau, Slade and Heathcote? Should we expect TIE to have evolved alongside the changing priorities of current thinking in education, or should it have the more provocative role of re-establishing a more holistic approach to education in schools? Ultimately, should TIE be evolving to adapt to its environment or seeking to change that environment? This is essentially a political question the answer to which will be predicated upon one's analysis of the current workings and functions of the education system. It is, though, a question that TIE companies are implicitly having to confront, even if they decline to do so explicitly. To disregard the issue involves accepting the status quo. Formerly DIE and TIE considered themselves as the potential hub of the educational wheel, offering coherence and relevance to schooling. It was an ambition unlikely ever to be achieved, but the question is now whether all such potential has been abandoned in favour of using DIE and TIE in the service of delivering aspects of the curriculum which are otherwise problematical. If this is happening, then current TIE theory may be suffering from an absence of philosophy. However, contemporary developments could also merely be associated with the pedestrian fact of financial pressure that requires it to respond to the needs of the education market.

Upon the evidence of current TIE practice in Wales, there seems little doubt that a change has occurred in the last fifteen years. Projects are generally shorter, more performance-based and are less likely to contain workshop elements. 'Actor/teachers' have become 'actors' and the educational significance of their work is more likely to be left to the teacher in the school to extract, though usually with the help of a resource pack. If there is a workshop it is as likely to consist of a discussion as a practical session, and as early as 1976 O'Toole had noted that 'in my experience, discussion in the most over-rated and unsatisfactory form of participation'.[6] No company in Wales has a core team of actors, though many use extended contracts and employ actors with previous experience of working in TIE. The TIE methodologies employed are largely in the hands of the artistic directors most of whom form the only link with 'traditional' TIE experience. It is certainly the case that all art forms evolve and develop and it should not surprise us that even directors who have been working in TIE for 30 years are not using the same approaches as they were at the beginning of their careers.

To further develop the conceit of evolutionary theory, the 'creature' that is TIE has had to adapt to survive the changes in the financial and educational environment. It can be argued, however, that the financial environment, at least in Wales, is more secure that it has ever been. Since the blossoming of TIE in the halcyon days of the 1960s and 1970s, the economic pressures upon education and the arts have been relentless with very few periods of expansion. This has pressurized companies to reassess their contractual arrangements, the duration of projects and the size of teams. The outcome of the Funding Agreement [2003] appears to offer a security to TIE in Wales which may yet turn out to be transient, even illusory, but the eight companies do enjoy a commitment from the Welsh Assembly Government and ACW, which earlier generations of TIE companies would envy. Inequalities in funding and disparities in levels of 'partnership' funding continue to exist, and cases where local authority officials turn first to arts organizations when seeking financial savings will undoubtedly persist. Generally, though, it cannot be argued that companies have had to alter their educational philosophy in order to survive. It is clear from the interviews with directors that the current methodologies are not generally the result of funding levels, but a matter of policy. At the same time, it may well be the case that the slow attrition of financial pressure over the years has gradually influenced what the companies feel able to achieve. Under constant pressure to 'prove their worth' and demonstrate 'value for money' it is possible that, over time, companies have increased their willingness to accept large audiences and to restrict the duration of programmes. This impacts upon the ability to offer workshops and/or participatory approaches. If this is the case, then younger members of the teams will not be aware of other ways of working, such knowledge residing in the artistic directors.

This lack of awareness about TIE methodology is, on the face of it, somewhat unexpected. Many drama schools, universities and even a few teacher-training establishments offer modules in DIE and TIE. Even at Level Three, Edexel's BTEC Performing Arts courses have available specialist units in both TIE and Theatre for Children. It might be expected therefore that aspiring actors will at least have the opportunity for basic training in both TIE and CT and be able to discern the differences between the two. However, the course content for these units is cited here as an example of the misunderstanding and obfuscation at work. The BTEC unit on Theatre for Children indicates that students should create theatre that 'educates', and gives the examples of 'bullying, information/awareness eg road safety, develop/ elaborate national curriculum'.[7]

Amongst the appropriate material for TIE, on the other hand, is 'curriculum development… road safety, drug and alcohol abuse [and] health and safety'.[8] At no point do students have to demonstrate an awareness or competence of even basic workshop or participatory methods. For BTEC Children's Theatre and TIE have become almost synonymous.

It was not initially envisaged that training for TIE would form a significant part of this study. However, it proved to be an issue of central concern to many companies. The perceived inadequacy of training reinforces this lack of knowledge of TIE technique. Several directors pointed out that most newly qualified actors have little if any methodological understanding of previous TIE theories. This, along with the demise of the 'core company', limits the extent to which expertise can be developed and bequeathed; there is neither the time in schools, nor the company expertise to work with the participatory methods of the past. The crucial issue here is whether, training and funding restraints aside, the directors of companies aspire to a situation where they *could* devote more resources to developing 'traditional' skills and participatory working methods. From the responses to the interviews it appears that this is not the case. Few companies, despite the improvement in their financial security, aspired again to create core actor/teacher teams. *Arad Goch* is focussing on commissioning new writing, and others intend to extend the range of their work. No company has mentioned [aside from *Theatr Powys* who continue to work in this way] a desire to use financial growth to develop more participatory or full-day projects. It could be extrapolated therefore that companies are largely content with the methodologies currently being used and that funding is not perceived to be a factor that has influenced the praxis of the work except marginally.

The second environmental change that TIE has had to survive is that within the educational system. After an increasingly child-centred approach throughout the growth of the state education system, the period since 1990 has arguably taken a completely different direction with 'training' for business and industry being elevated above holistic education and the development of life skills. Whilst there is little doubt that the work of the TIE companies in Wales displays high levels of theatrical skill, creativity and artistic challenge, it is no longer clear that educational objectives and teleology are clearly defined. Educationally the work is generally respected, welcomed and well used by the schools, but does not appear to have the same foundation of pedagogic rigour that might have once been the case. It is the case that in Wales the drama legacy of Heathcote, Bolton and others was never as deeply rooted as elsewhere in Britain, largely because of the preference to seek non-English sources of inspiration. For many companies, therefore, current praxis displays no major shift away from a TIE paradigm that they did not endorse in the first instance and which has historically caused rifts between Wales' companies. In the 1980s, for example, many companies in Wales refused to ally themselves to the *Standing Conference of Young People's Theatre* on both political and methodological grounds. Thus the differences between Children's Theatre, TIE and Educational Theatre, outlined above, would not have been accepted by many in Wales.

It is arguable that throughout the history of the TIE movement in Wales, programmes have always had more of an emphasis on performance than was generally the case in Britain as a whole; there have always been different approaches to, and interpretations of, the praxis. However, as has been shown, the defining characteristics of TIE in Wales have not historically differed markedly from those in the English tradition. In this context it is worth noting again the comments of Savill, herself a Welsh TIE director and commentator:

> TIE aims to enable children to learn through experience which is stimulated and motivated by theatre… [The] audience will be assigned a specific role which enables them to react and interact without the burden of self-consciousness.[9]

She goes on to define TIE as 'essentially heuristic. The audience are given the role of investigators and are released by this into a process of discovery'.[10] These remarks were made in 1988, the year of ERA, and demonstrate that at this point in the TIE movement, the aims and aspirations of TIE in Wales were not perceived to be educationally distinct from those in England. Thus, though TIE may never have been the same creature as it was elsewhere in Britain, the educational imperatives, based upon the universality of a child's need to make meaning of the world, are congruent. With its distinct cultural heritage, no art form emerging in Wales should be expected to mirror that of England, but the basic tenets of education, and thus TIE, remain the same; that 'the audience should be challenged to participate rather than absorb solutions.'[11]

The question that must be confronted is whether TIE in Wales today is serving a purpose that is anything more than a provision of theatrical experience for children in schools. Ultimately the answer must be in the affirmative, for all companies are well able to justify their work in terms of legitimate educational outcomes. However, the nature of TIE is under a severe threat of dilution since the underpinning drama education praxis is, with the exception of *Theatr Powys*, clearly less valued. This reflects the fact that notions of child-centred learning, cross-curriculum work and the importance of reflection are less cherished in education today. Again we see that TIE has evolved to fit current requirements. Perhaps, though, the evidence suggests that this evolution has reached the point where it has become a new species and not TIE at all.

As has been shown, most companies are proud of the relationship they have with schools and with the education establishment. Further, they believe they are responding to children's needs every bit as much as were early proponents of TIE. This is to define the needs of children within the accepted epistemology of current education. If contemporary educational structures and systems are a paradigm, then it is to be welcomed that TIE has so aptly adapted to answer these needs. If, however, the actual needs of children were misidentified by ERA and after, it would be the case that TIE is failing to offer the holistic educational and child-centred alternative approach that, along with DIE, it had proved itself able to provide. The ability of TIE/DIE to nourish the development of the whole child and to offer contextualization of a confusing world, remain unique. If the progressive educationalists of the 1960s, 1970s and 1980s were right in this, then it may be that TIE still has a unique responsibility to meet that demand despite the strictures of curriculum. The research accompanying this study has shown that few contemporary actor/teachers [or 'actors working in TIE'] are from the world of education. At the same time, schools are increasing served by teachers who have little theoretical knowledge of pre-ERA ideas of progressive and heuristic education. It may therefore be regarded as a positive factor that TIE workers are coming from outside this narrow educational world, since they are better able to offer new perspectives on learning and can offer an additional dimension to current work in schools. They are only able to do this, however, if they can gain access to the classroom. This implies an educational 'bind', for to gain access to schools TIE is increasingly expected to be able to serve the needs of teachers and their delivery of the National Curriculum. Ogden predicts, in 1997, that companies would come under pressure to play to large audiences, deal with set texts and charge schools.[12] This appears to be a prophesy that has come to pass, and it seems to be the case that TIE companies in Wales are having to gain access to schools by persuading teachers that the work can serve the curriculum needs of the school. At the same time they hope that they can achieve their own, wider, educational objectives. This is what Baker is referring to when he cites the case of gaining access to schools to undertake a project about World War Two in order to work with the children on the issue of truth and lies in families.[13] In this way companies can be seen to be responding to Pammenter's exhortation that 'TIE teams have a responsibility to the education system but a greater responsibility to the children.'[14]

The purpose of educating the 'whole child' and encouraging the ability to reflect and question, it will be remembered, was to empower the child to 'make meaning' and to contemplate the possibility of change.[15] It is arguable that such goals are no longer valued within education perhaps reflecting the situation in contemporary society at large. Such political ambitions have been replaced in recent years by the need to address personal and social behaviour through the PSHE curriculum. Once again, it must be considered whether TIE is correct to abandon the former DIE/TIE concepts of 'universals' and an empathetic understanding of the world and replace them with the skills of observation and objective discussion. The social learning needs of the child have become personalized rather than universalized, and TIE appears to be adapting to these requirements. After fourteen years of the National Curriculum, the education system appears to be finding that narrow Learning Objectives are insufficient to deal with the wider needs of children. Holt points out than within a curriculum the one millionth of human knowledge that we learn might not be the right one millionth.[16] The potential education from drama and TIE can focus on giving the life skills that we all know we will all need. These skills are now narrowly defined by the expanding PSHE curriculum, the creation of a Citizenship Curriculum and increasing teacher appeals for help in dealing with issues such as bullying, drugs, alcohol and abuse. These were once the natural fuel of the drama lesson since they revolve around issues of responsibility and empathy. Such issues could be felt subjectively, reflected upon, and analysed objectively through drama – and through 'traditional' TIE. The need is still there, and indeed growing, and much of the TIE analysed for this research responds to these issues. At the same time, however, TIE has evolved in another direction and now inhabits the educational territory where the tendency is to tell and test. '[TIE's] midwife and its testing ground is the era in which it lives', wrote Baskerville in 1973.[17] The defining participatory format, identified, for example, by Eileen Murphy in 1975,[18] has all but disappeared. It is now more common for children to be asked, in discussion, what they thought the 'play' was about rather than be involved in any empathetic or reflective consideration of the themes. Possibly we are seeing the end of Brecht's 'scientific world' where reflection leading to action was the legitimate goal. Perhaps we now inhabit a post-theoretical world where 'what is' remains unchallenged; where the political and educational consensus cannot not be disturbed. Esslin points out that 'drama in performance is human life put on a pedestal to be exhibited, looked at, examined and contemplated'.[19] Increasingly it seems that whilst this pedestal is being used to exhibit human life, the opportunity to contemplate, to reflect, is being overlooked by contemporary TIE in Wales. The essential element of 'learning through experience'[20] has seemingly been removed from the process.

It is important to reiterate that all the projects seen for this analysis had many fine qualities, especially in terms of performance and production values. It is also true, however, that 'traditional' TIE approaches have been transformed and even abandoned. It appears that this transformation has been in response to a variety of pressures including, but not restricted to, the demands of a National Curriculum. TIE has changed to meet these needs and in doing so much of the work would not fit the criteria for TIE set out by earlier commentators, though much of it has substantial educational value. It is argued, however, that TIE in Wales has done more than evolve to adapt to the changing financial and educational environment. Rather, it has mutated into a new creature that primarily aims to offer a strong theatrical stimulus to schools and, incidentally, offers the wily teacher the opportunity to use the work in the Core and PSHE curricula. This applies to different degrees to different companies and those who have 'mutated' furthest from TIE precepts will readily accept the fact. At least two companies in Wales no longer use 'TIE' in their title and even more question the relevance of the term to their work. Few companies use the title 'actor/teacher'. The work they take to schools is still highly valuable since they are offering an educational input that adds depth and resonance to an otherwise overly narrow curriculum. Indeed, for most, adherence to Curriculum needs is not an issue. However, the original precepts of TIE are rarely to be seen and for that reason the process, since 1988, can be regarded as one of mutation into a form of Educational Theatre, rather than the evolution of a progressive and child-centred theatre and education praxis.

Notes

1. BASKERVILLE, R. op. cit., p. 7.
2. ITZIN, C. op. cit., p. xii.
3. Appendix Three, p. 106.
4. SCYPT Journal 13, London, SCYPT, 1984, p. 4.
5. Appendix Three, pp. 143.
6. O'TOOLE, J. op. cit., p. 88.
7. EDEXCEL, *Level 3 Nationals in Performing Arts, Guidance and Units*, 2002, p. 144.
8. Ibid., p. 138.
9. SAVILL, C. C. op. cit., p. 49.
10. Ibid., p. 50.
11. OGDEN, G. in A-M. TAYLOR (ed.), op. cit., p. 53.
12. Ibid., p. 59.
13. See Appendix Three, p. 131.
14. PAMMENTER, D. in T. JACKSON, op. cit., p. 63.
15. See REDINGTON, C. op. cit., chapter 1.
16. HOLT, J. op. cit., p. 292.
17. BASKERVILLE, R. op. cit., p. 11.
18. MURPHY, E. op. cit., p. 5.
19. ESSLIN, M. *The Field of Drama*, London, Methuen, 1987, p. 39.
20. SCHWEITZER, P. (ed.), op. cit., p. 7.

Appendix One

The Companies, the Projects and the Interviewees

Arad Goch

Stryd y Baddon

Aberystwyth

SY23 2NN

Title of Project:	O Fore Gwyn Tan Nos		
Visited:	23/06/04	**Venue:** Ysgol Pontyberen	
Interviewee:	Jeremy Turner	**Date:** 16/12/04	

Cwmni'r Frân Wen.

Y Hen Ysgol Gynradd

Ffordd Pentraeth

Porthaethwy

Ynys Môn

Gwynedd

LL59 5HS

Title of Project:	Lleisiau yn y Parc		
Visited:	24/06/04	**Venue:** Ysgol Pontyberen	
Interviewee:	Iola Ynyr [by e-mail]	**Date:** received 17/12/04	

Gwent Theatre

Drama Centre

Pen-y-Pound

Abergavenny

Gwent

NP7 5UD

Title of Project: Home Front
Visited: 11/06/04   **Venue:** Llangynidr C.P. School
Interviewees: Gary Meredith and Jain Boon   **Date:** 28/06/04

Theatr Iolo Ltd.,

The Old School Building

Cefn Road

Mynachdy

Cardiff

CF14 3HS

Title of Project: The Journey
Visited: 01/07/04   **Venue:** Coryton C.P. School
Interviewee: Kevin Lewis   **Date:** 01/07/04

Theatr Na n'Og

Uned 3,

Ystad Ddiwydiannol

Heol Millands

Castell Nedd

SA11 1NJ

Title of Project: Big Bad Wolf
Visited: 30/06/04   **Venue:** Coedffranc C.P. School
Interviewee: Rachel Clancy   **Date:** 30/06/04

[further information received by e-mail from Geinor Jones 6/07/04]

Spectacle Theatre

Rhondda College

Llwynpia

Tonypandy

CF40 2TQ

Title of Project: Where's Andy?
Visited: 28/06/04   **Venue:** Cwmbach Infant School
Interviewee: Steve Davies [by e-mail]   **Date received:** 15/11/04

<u>Theatr Clwyd Young People's Theatre</u>

County Civic Centre

Mold

Clwyd

CH7 1YA

Title of Project: The Mabinogion
Visited: 16/06/04   **Venue:** Theatr Clywd
Interviewee: Tim Baker   **Date:** 16/06/04

<u>Theatr Powys</u>

Tremont Road

Llandrindod

LD1 5EB

Title of Project: Pow Wow
Visited: 14/06/04   **Venue:** Treowen C.P. School
Interviewee: Ian Yeoman   **Date:** 20/08/04

The Questionnaire

At the outset of this research into current TIE practice in Wales it seemed appropriate that not only should the programmes themselves be observed, but that also the directors of the companies should be given the opportunity to contextualize the work within the wider framework of the companies' aims and objectives. Clearly it was possible that any specific piece of work might not reflect the overall style and educational approach of the company and therefore it would be necessary to investigate the policies of the companies more widely in order that valid conclusions might be drawn.

The questions were thus drawn up with the aim of investigating a wide range of areas that might reflect educational and artistic policies. These covered areas of educational objectives and liaison with schools, the use of workshops and participatory approaches, drama and theatre influences on the work, recruitment policies and financial security. There were also questions about any wider remit that the company might have including INSET training, community and youth theatre work. As the focus of the research became clearer this final set of questions impacted less on the developing analyses, as did questions about the primary/secondary balance of work and the number of projects undertaken each year. However, all these responses are recorded in the transcriptions of the full interviews reproduced in Appendix Three and summarized in Table I.

A draft questionnaire was drawn up, and, in order not to 'contaminate' responses to the actual interviewing process with Wales' companies, Chris Cooper at *Big Brum TIE* was approached and agreed to undertake the interview and to give comments on the questions and structure of the process. This led to several adjustments to the questions aimed at clarifying their purpose and for which the author is very grateful.

On the advice of Chris Cooper, an additional question was added to those in the original draft which proved to be crucial in eliciting information about the way in which companies considered their own work and responsibilities. Following the question about the way in which companies worked with schools, Cooper suggested the inclusion of a question about the *extent to which companies considered the needs of children*. This enabled the questions to identify more clearly the consideration of the needs of education 'suppliers' and education 'consumers' separately.

The interviews were carried out as soon as possible following the observation of the TIE programme. In most cases this was within a few weeks, but in some cases a longer interval occurred due to the proximity of the summer vacation period. The interview with *Arad Goch*, for example, did not take place until nearly six months following the viewing of the project. In two further cases [*Cwmni'r Frân Wen* and *Spectacle Theatre*] it proved impossible to schedule an interview, and here the directors completed answers to the questionnaire via e-mail. The answers in these cases understandably tended to be more succinct. Further clarification of their responses was undertaken by telephone where necessary. The interview with *Theatr Na n'Og* was carried out immediately after the performance with the Education Officer, and was noted by hand. These notes were then typed up and sent to the director who added further information. The two different respondents are identified in the transcription below. *Gwent Theatre* also offered two interviewees, the director of the project and the Artistic Director of the company. In this case too the two respondents are identified in the transcription. Other than *Frân Wen*, *Spectacle* and *Theatr Na n'Og*, all the interviews were audio recorded and generally lasted between an hour and ninety minutes. The responses were later transcribed and are reproduced in full.

Interview Questionnaire

Interview Questions for Research into Current TIE Practice in Wales

Name of Company.......................... **Title of project**...............................
Date of Visit.......... **Name of Interviewee**................... **Position**................
Duration of Project.......................... [**Performance**....... **Workshop**.........]

1. *How would you define the Educational Aim of the project?*
2. *How was the project devised or developed?*
3. *How many performances of the project are planned?*
4. *Do you ever re-tour projects? Under what circumstances?*
5. *To what extent were teachers involved in the choice of material or the development of ideas?*
6. *Does the company attempt to identify the needs of the children when developing projects?*
7. *How would you describe your relationship with schools and what developments would you like to see?*
8. *Do you employ a 'schools liaison' officer and what are the duties of this post?*
9. *Do you provide teaching materials/teaching packs and how are these compiled?*
10. *Does the project have identified links to Learning Objectives of the National Curriculum?*
11. *Did the project include workshop or participatory elements? YES/NO*

    If yes, what governed the choice of methodologies?

    If no, why was the decision made not to use participatory elements?
12. *Do you have a policy about the use of workshop and/or participatory work?*
13. *What theatrical influences currently affect your performance work?*
14. *What drama influences currently affect your participatory work?*
15. *What do you feel are the key differences between Theatre for Children and Theatre in Education?*
16. *Are your current actors specifically trained/experienced in TIE?*
17. *Is training or experience in drama/TIE an employment criterion when making acting appointments?*
18. *Are any of your actors teacher trained? Would this be an advantage?*

19. *In what ways has TIE practice in your company changed or developed in recent years?*

20. *How confident are you about the future of TIE in Wales?*

21. *How confident are you about the future of your company?*

22. *In percentage terms what are your sources of funding?*

23. *Do you work in both primary and secondary schools? What is the percentage split between the two sectors?*

24. *How many TIE projects does the company undertake each year?*

25. *Is your company also involved in community or other forms of theatre?*

26. *Is your company involved in INSET training for teachers?*

27. *Do you have any further reflections on the current state of TIE in Wales?*

Appendix Three

The Interviews

Name of Company: *Arad Goch*   **Title of project:** *O Fore Gwyn Tan Nos*
Date of Visit: 30/06/04 **Interviewee**: Jeremy Turner **Position:** Artistic Director
Duration of Project: 65 minutes [Performance 45 Workshop 20]

1. How would you define the Educational Aim of the project?

The first thing to say that is that in *Arad Goch* the emphasis is on 'theatre' in 'theatre in education'. Though we do refer to the Curriculum, the impetus for our work comes always from the artist rather than from the curriculum needs. Having said that, we discuss our work with teachers and different Advisors to ensure that our work is of use and of relevance to them as well. The educational aim of *O Fore Gwyn Tan Nos*, if you want to put it into a Curriculum context, was to do with the PSHE curriculum. The initial idea was mine and it was about children not being able to make decisions: worrying about having to make decisions. I probably thought about this because I have two children of my own, and having been through the traumas with them – what they are going to wear each day, who they are going to play with and this, that and the other – things which to us, as adults, are petty and irrelevant, but which to kids are very, very big, major decisions. Unless they can talk about the problem and work through the problem then it can boil and fester. So very simply it was about that.

2. How was the project devised or developed?

After I had the initial idea, I met with the three actors who were going to take part in it long before we started the actual formal rehearsal period. We met for a weekend initially, to talk about my ideas and for them to throw ideas back at me. Then we met a couple of months later for two weeks and looked at the ideas more closely and developed some of them. We played with various techniques – with dance, with music, poetry – but still we didn't structure the play. We just played. I then sent them all away with a disposable camera and asked them to take pictures over the coming five weeks of life from the perspective of a five-year-old. And I sort of knew what would happen, but it informed them about the way that children see the world. All that was before we had a four-week rehearsal period.

3. How many performances of the project are planned?

Loads [consults computer]. About… I think it was ninety-nine performances.

4. Do you ever re-tour projects? Under what circumstances?

Yes. If I think a project is good – if we get a good response to it from the schools – we'll wrap it up for a year or two and then re-tour it. We invest so much in the work, not just financially but artistically, and I think it only right that we make the most of the ideas that we've got. Sometimes there might be a problem getting the same cast together and then we'll bring someone new in. We've done that very often.

5. To what extent were teachers involved in the choice of material or the development of ideas?

We try to meet annually with two of the Education Officers and we talk with them about the year plan and about whether we want to focus on particular projects. They very seldom question our work now because we've built up a long-term relationship with them. They trust us and the teachers trust us, which is good. But it's also not so good because sometimes we need a dialogue – to throw the ideas around and wash them out a bit. With this particular project, for part of the preparation period, I sent the actors into schools for a few days each, for them to see the children and listen to them. They could also talk to the teachers about the ideas we had. There was a lot of on-site discussion in a way. Sometimes if a show is particularly sensitive we make sure that all teachers know about its sensitivity. It varies from project to project.

6. Does the company attempt to identify the needs of the children when developing projects?

Yes, partly through personal experience. But it's also happened (especially with older children over the last six years) because we've been working with groups of what are known as 'disaffected youths': young people who've been thrown out of school. We've worked with them and their teachers and the pupil referral unit and their social workers on seven-week projects: they come to us one day a week for six weeks and, then, the seventh week, they work with us for a whole week to create a piece of theatre – possibly the first piece of theatre that they've created – and probably the first time they've been applauded for anything. We started this about six years ago. It was partnership which the WJEC set up called '*The Artisan Project*'. I was very sceptical about it, and it didn't work as well as it should have. The proviso I gave was that we entered into it on the understanding that we, as professionals, would get something out of it, not just to be generous and altruistic. And we did get a lot out of it. It informed our professional practise and the way we think about putting work together – especially for teenagers. And we still work with those groups of young people. Very often they still call in to see where they were and bring their friends with them. Following one of the projects we set up a scheme with two of the young people who were interested in writing. They created their own script under our leadership, which we produced with a professional cast. And we sometimes bring some of these young people in to help us discuss or to analyse scripts before we go into production and they tell us 'no, that's not right, they wouldn't f*cking say that'. This is an informal arrangement. The kids aren't a panel. They are just young people on whose expertise and experience we can call.

7. How would you describe your relationship with schools and what developments would you like to see?

It's difficult. Schools are so busy and the demands on teachers and the pupils are so heavy. We'd all like to see more art in schools, and it does happen depending upon the priorities of the teachers and the head teachers. There are some very, very good schools which do almost no theatre work apart from the school pantomime. There are others where pupils get a lot of arts activity. It's not my place to say really. I'd like there to be some sort of recognition of arts activity in schools and more encouragement of arts activity: for children to encounter live arts in an active/participatory way and in a passive way as members of an audience. In this county, in Ceredigion, we get to each school at least once a year if not twice. We service three counties since Dyfed was split up – Ceredigion, Carmarthen and Pembrokeshire – and each of those counties has a different way of funding us. So the uptake in each of those counties is different depending on how big the funding is.

One more thing – we often ask the Education Advisors what their educational priorities are for the next two or three years. And if we can, we respond to them. Not slavishly – if we can respond to them and integrate what their priorities are into what we want to do, then we will.

8. Do you employ a 'schools liaison' officer and what are the duties of this post?

We employ a marketing officer, and she has the overall responsibility of setting up tours with schools. She is not a trained teacher though she has taught in Further Education and has worked in a number of academic institutions. We also have on the staff two trained teachers who are performers and one is a writer as well. Between those three people we have got a lot of experience of working with schools.

9. Do you provide teaching materials/teaching packs and how are these compiled?

Yes. Usually this is something that the director would do. They are usually compiled as the project develops. We have moved in recent years from packs which have a lot of background material for teachers, towards packs which have more readily usable ideas and tasks that teachers use with the children. More user-friendly, user-ready. As a result they are now much better used than they used to be.

10. Does the project have identified links to Learning Objectives of the National Curriculum?

I suppose I should say 'yes'! Our way of working is that we refer to the Curriculum – and we know the Curriculum quite well – but once we've started work on a show, it is only after we've had the initial idea that we turn to the Curriculum to see where we could use the Curriculum as a 'coat hanger' and say that 'this show will cover nineteenth-century Wales and topics of travelling' and so on. It is always that way round.

11. Did the project include workshop or participatory elements? YES/NO

If yes, what governed the choice of methodologies?

We started work with *Arad Goch* fifteen years ago and made the decision that we'd separate the performance aspects of the work from the interactive elements of the work. So almost all of our works in schools are straight performances. No interaction. The interactive element comes after the performance – a workshop or practical discussion with the actors and the children.

If no, why was the decision made not to use participatory elements?

12. Do you have a policy about the use of workshop and/or participatory work?

It's not strict policy, but that's the way we prefer to work rather than create what some people call 'traditional' theatre in education. I don't think there is any more such a thing as traditional TIE. I'm not sure that there ever was. There was a way of working that some companies used. But I don't think that that is the only TIE pattern. There were other patterns even in the early days. As I said before, our emphasis is on the theatrical: if the theatre's good, the education's good. If the theatre's crap, the education will be crap. I have seen so many performances which try to be highly educative but actually they turn off some children.

13. What theatrical influences currently affect your performance work?

My early work, before I started work in children's theatre, was heavily informed by the work of Grotowski and Barba and various other European companies, and that was probably because when I was here in college in the 70s, I saw a lot of the works by the groups that were then in Cardiff. New experimental groups like *Cardiff Lab* and *Paupers Carnival* and Jeff Moore's work. That made me realize that there was a new way of creating Welsh theatre, Welsh-language theatre, that wasn't a slavish carbon copy of English middle-of-the-road theatre. It's ironic now that we've just re-established a National Welsh language theatre – an idea that everybody had hoped for and thought was dead forever! The Phoenix has arisen! I used to work for a company called *Cwmni Cyfri Tri*, which was an experimental independent company which did exactly what it wanted to. It was set up as a three-month project and it lasted for nine years. Fair play to the *Welsh Arts Council* [as it was then], they let us carry on for nine years because, I hope, the work was good and very different from anything else being produced in Wales at the time; it was new work and it was challenging and it was in Welsh. The company became too small and the other company in Aberystwyth at the time, *Theatr Crwban* [a TIE company], was also too small to be viable financially and artistically. I was persuaded by the Arts Council to consider merging the two companies. My dread was that I would end up doing… naff kid's work which would not enable me to continue the experimental work that I'd been doing. So I was sent by the Arts Council to various festivals abroad, and the work of a number of companies in a number of countries influenced me – especially working in Belgium and in Denmark where children's theatre is still free theatre. It still has close links with abstract and visual experimental theatre. I think that in Britain those new strands of theatre were separated very quickly in the 70s. Experimental theatre became very, very experimental and self-indulgent and TIE work became slightly 'Blue Peter', 'this is good for you children'. On the continent, in a number of countries, the principles and the power and the impetus of '66, '67, '69 is still there. The work continues to be fresh, even though most of the people working in those countries are older than me. And they have the same fears as me – that there is no one behind me to kick my arse as I once kicked arses. We should be pensioned off, I think! That would do theatre in Wales a lot of good, I think – if they pensioned us all off!

But, no, Belgian and Danish work have been a key influence. French work tends to be very, very philosophical. Some German work I like, but mainly Belgian.

14. What drama influences currently affect your participatory work?

What do you mean? Like Heathcote? Those ideas are there – they've always been there. But we don't refer to them as a matter of policy. The work of Heathcote and Bolton has been taken by everybody differently and developed in different ways. Each to their own inspiration and desire and aims. The first aim of our workshops is to bridge between the work that the children have just seen and their everyday school lives. A lot of teachers ask us, 'can we do drama work with the children – acting?'. But we can't do an acting workshop with 30 children in an hour with the dinner ladies clattering the pots and pans. So, we say, 'no', but what we do try to do is to set the children topics and themes or just touch on some of the themes of the play. So they are not just left stranded thinking 'that was good', and that's it. They are given a bit of a prod after the play. And for these children – five- and six-year-olds – this will be a very gentle prod. For them to realize, and to consider without realizing it, that they are thinking about some of the things that went on in the play.

15. What do you feel are the key differences between Theatre for Children and Theatre in Education?

Theatre for Children is like you or I going to the theatre to see a good play and be informed by it. We enjoy it. It's a good night or afternoon. In the same way children have the need and the right to see such work without it having to be educative. Half of our work is Theatre for Young Audiences, outside school time, outside the school walls, outside the curriculum. The other half is what we call TIE. Some of the purists wouldn't call it TIE, but I do. This work is somehow linked to their work in schools. You saw a piece of work [*O Fore Gwyn Tan Nos – From Dawn to Dusk*] which we hang on the PSHE curriculum, language, music and visual arts. But there have been a number of our pieces, for junior schools, for instance, which are history plays – not because we thought, 'right we must do a history play for the National Curriculum', but because one of our writers likes writing history plays and she enjoys the research process – losing herself in the National Library of Wales for a couple of months! And that is obviously very, very useful for Curriculum work. Very often teachers only think that there are one or two main themes to a piece of work. We once did a play which dealt with mid-nineteenth-century Wales, Victorian Britain, travelling and the Americas. There was a whole raft of themes. I made a spider chart for teachers with themes and sub-themes and sub-themes to sub-themes. I think there were a hundred and twenty-five elements from which every teacher could think, 'oh, right, that's relevant to what I'm doing this term'. We don't do that for every play, but it was an exercise to demonstrate to myself and the teachers the scope of any piece of work.

16. Are your current actors specifically trained/experienced in TIE?

No. They are good actors. I mentioned already that we have two actresses and teachers, and one has worked only in TIE. The others work in TIE and main stage. Because of the crossover of work in Wales, we are still lucky with actors who do a bit of television, do their *Pobl Y Cwm**, do a bit of main stage work and they are still willing to do TIE.

17. Is training or experience in drama/TIE an employment criterion when making acting appointments?

No. No. It's not. They have to be good actors. One of the elements of Barba's work and Grotowski's work that has influenced us and is one of our principles is the principle of continual training. An actor never finishes learning his craft. So a lot of our work is training work, in what we call stage technique. This is not carried out in a formal or formalistic way. We are always trying to find new potential within ourselves. When we have new actors who are not experienced in TIE we take specific care to brief them and to introduce them to the 'dos and don'ts' and the potential of TIE. 'Induction', I suppose, is the word.

18. Are any of your actors teacher trained? Would this be an advantage?

We don't have a permanent team of actors. We don't call them actor/teachers. It is an advantage to have trained teachers on the team. They can speak the same jargon as the teachers.

19. In what ways has TIE practice in your company changed or developed in recent years?

It's become more script-based over the last five years. That is maybe because it is easier to commission a script and to work through that script and then put it into production. It takes longer but it is easier than devising a piece. Devising a piece is such an intricate process because you are working with more than one mind. And because our turnover is quite rapid – up to eight productions a year – we've had to use scripts for a number of those productions. That's not a bad thing, but sometimes one wishes for more time to devise because that's where I started really. Having said that, we have recently commissioned seven new scripts. We had new money from the Arts Council two years ago (which we had to spend in four months, I think) and a big part of it we spent commissioning seven new scripts which will be developed over the next three years. Some are from people experienced in writing for children and some from experienced writers who have never written for children. We are developing their skills as well.

20. How confident are you about the future of TIE in Wales?

Until last week [w/b 6/12/04] I was very confident. Rhodri Morgan [First Minister of Welsh Assembly Government] said he was taking care of the big companies, the big boys, and he was leaving all the rest to the Arts Council. That might suggest that the decision of the Arts Council in London this week to give more money to national galleries and less money to regional work and to new work, might be the reason that Rhodri Morgan took the big companies under his wing, I don't know, but I wouldn't be surprised; maybe I'm too cynical. I think we are fairly safe, fairly safe, but I think that the change in emphasis in government thinking – not in Arts Council thinking but in government thinking – is towards 'flagships'. And I think that that's one of the negative effects of Devolution, which I've always been in favour of. But it's a negative effect because the politicians who were small politicians in the British pond are now bigger politicians in the Welsh pond. And they want something to wave around. They are looking for the things to boast about. One of them said that TIE is 'the jewel in the Welsh crown' – but they don't actually polish it too often.

21. How confident are you about the future of your company?

There is no reason not to be confident. There is a big capital project at the moment to expand the company's base. We are moving out of this building for a year and a half in order to rebuild within the walls of these buildings.

22. In percentage terms what are your sources of funding?

I suppose it is about 65 per cent from the Arts Council, maybe 10 per cent or 20 per cent from the Local Authorities and the rest from Box office, fees and sponsorship.

23. Do you work in both primary and secondary schools? What is the percentage split between the two sectors?

We try to do one project a year for each of the four Key Stages. This is what we and the other seven TIE companies and the Arts Council decided to set as an aim over the next seven years. We weren't very far off it actually. We used to do one project for secondary schools a year, and this last year we've done two projects. It has been an experiment to start with to see if we and the secondary schools could cope with two secondary school projects in a year. It's difficult because the timetable in secondary schools is so busy and so full and so inflexible. Key Stage Three we are coping with well, but Key Stage Four is more difficult to get access to unless we do a set text, which we try not to do. Our tours to junior schools are much longer than our tours to secondary schools.

24. How many TIE projects does the company undertake each year?

Four or five.

25. Is your company also involved in community or other forms of theatre?

Yes. We do one project a year for children under eleven which goes into theatres and arts centres. And we do one project a year for young people which will go into community venues and theatres. Usually there's another project – a gap in the programme which enables us to do something different.

26. Is your company involved in INSET training for teachers?

Yes, in a number of forms. Before a TIE tour we offer a teachers' preview, but these are attended less and less. I take this to be a good sign, a sign that the teachers trust us. We have worked with the three Education Authorities in Ceredigion, Carmarthenshire and Pembrokeshire and with Education Authorities outside our own TIE patch more and more over the last five or six years providing training in a number of different elements. The use of theatre is one, the use of theatre for language teaching is another. We actively looked for opportunities five years ago to plug into this because we know that our work has a longer after-effect if the teachers feel confident with it. Since we made that initial advance five years ago, it's not something we *look* for every year, but it is something that comes our way in different forms each year. We attempt to help overcome the lack of Welsh language expertise or expertise by people who can speak Welsh, in different parts of the country.

The training of actors for this type of work is an issue for us. There is not one course in Wales which adequately trains actors to work in TIE. There are various modules, but I don't think you can teach TIE in a seven-week module. Unfortunately, in some colleges the model of TIE that is taught is based very much on what is perceived to be by some the traditional TIE mould, which I think is wrong. I get very angry when I see students being forced to devise a piece of TIE themselves with very, very little leadership. Then they are expected to take that piece of TIE into schools. I don't think it is fair on the students and it is very, very unfair and dangerous for the school children. They wouldn't be asked to produce a piece of Shakespeare with no leadership or with their peers acting as directors using the old, so-called 'traditional TIE devisory' process. If you want to teach students what TIE is, that is exactly the wrong way to do it, because they need the expertise of a professional to know what TIE is. It is such a delicate and sensitive area.

27. Do you have any further reflections on the current state of TIE in Wales?

Yes, I think that all of us ought to be pensioned off! Two of us each year. Most of us working in TIE now started when we were angry young things. We wanted to do something different. That's how it was for me. I wasn't interested in working with children when I started, I just wanted to do different theatre – different to the crap I was seeing. There are not that many angry young things out there now. Many of them come out of college with loans to pay off so they can't afford to bum around on a project grant or on their own money for a year and do their own thing. Very often when they do do that they are put up on a pedestal as the 'new hope', whereas we weren't put up on pedestals; we were told to 'f*ck off, don't bother us'! Being put up on those pedestals is very dangerous. They are not given the chance to fail. Also because companies are so intent on their own practices and philosophies, people perceive that there's no space within the scene. They have no idea what we've been trying to do – 'trying', I emphasize – to encourage people to come to us with their ideas. And if their ideas are workable – not necessarily good, but workable – we will try to put some of our resources behind them. This might be my time or a company member's time, rehearsal space, equipment or sometimes money – to help them develop new ideas. Then, very often, that means that they become too dependent on us. I want them to use us, not abuse us, to take us for granted. There is a danger that new ideas get adjusted to fit in with what it is perceived that we want, and then the newness of the ideas is lost.

I would also like to mention the international work. This has been a pretty big part of our work for a number of years since I started to see overseas work, and I came to realize that there is a lot of work in Wales that is of a higher standard than a lot of foreign work. Not all of it is of a high standard. When I try to persuade people from Canada or wherever to come and see Arad Goch's work, it's 'oh, we couldn't possibly.' They'll come to London or they'll come to Cardiff, but to come to the sticks north of the M4 is out of the question! That is why I set up the international festival, Agor Dsysau [www.agordrysau-openingdoors.org], which still happens, as a window of Welsh work and a bridge into and out of Wales. I think there is much more that we could do to 'sell' our work. There's a huge market out there. We need to be much more canny and businesslike than we are. We are still a bit settled into our traditional markets rather than saying, 'well, we've got all this expertise, we need to market it'. There's always a feeling that we are there on sufferance.

* *Pobl y Cwm* is a long-running, Welsh-language 'soap' broadcast on S4C, the Welsh Channel Four.

Name of Company: *Cwmni'r Frân Wen*   **Title of project:** *Lleisiau yn y Parc*
Date of Visit: 24/06/04   **Interviewee**: Iola Ynyr   **Position**: Director [via e-mail]
Duration of Project: 55 minutes [Performance 35   Workshops 20]

1. How would you define the Educational Aim of the project?

To promote understanding of how to form a friendship. To appreciate when a relationship is positive or harmful. To encourage respect towards others and to take responsibility for one's actions. To gain independence.

2. How was the project devised or developed?

The project was based on the book by Anthony Browne and was devised by Iola Ynyr after co-operating with Anthony.

3. How many performances of the project are planned?

The recent tour had 80 performances.

4. Do you ever re-tour projects? Under what circumstances?

This is the third tour of the project. Projects are re-toured if they are deemed successful by the company and schools.

5. To what extent were teachers involved in the choice of material or the development of ideas?

Questionnaires are given to teachers for suggested themes.

6. Does the company attempt to identify the needs of the children when developing projects?

This is done by teacher responses and curricular objectives.

7. How would you describe your relationship with schools and what developments would you like to see?

A healthy and open relationship exists with the schools which is formed by asking them to preview projects pre-touring. We invite comments on content, style, suitability and we give an introduction to the follow up activities in the work pack.

8. Do you employ a 'schools liaison' officer and what are the duties of this post?

Yes. She is responsible for the educational aspect of the projects such as assessing the suitability of projects, producing work packs and touring as a workshop facilitator.

9. Do you provide teaching materials/teaching packs and how are these compiled?

The work packs are based on the curricular objectives of the specific age group and usually follow the format of a synopsis, relevance to the Curriculum, cross-curricular activities, poetry and other relevant literature and a bibliography. Information regarding relevant agencies is also included.

10. Does the project have identified links to Learning Objectives of the National Curriculum?

As above.

11. Did the project include workshop or participatory elements? YES/NO

If yes, what governed the choice of methodologies?

The workshop encouraged discussion about gaining independence, relationships with parents and friends, self confidence, self esteem and creating a safe environment to express feelings and emotions.

If no, why was the decision made not to use participatory elements?

12. Do you have a policy about the use of workshop and/or participatory work?

Every workshop is tailored to the project's aims and demands. It might be the case that a workshop is unsuitable for a certain age group, size of audience or the actual content, therefore a workshop is not given. The comprehensive work pack produced is sufficient to initiate discussion and address any issues.

13. What theatrical influences currently affect your performance work?

Each project has its own theatrical style. However, all of the company's work aims to challenge the audience and show respect towards them.

14. What drama influences currently affect your participatory work?

The company has in the past had training by Dorothy Heathcote and admire her unpatronising approach towards children and young people.

15. What do you feel are the key differences between Theatre for Children and Theatre in Education?

Theatre in Education is based on an educational experience rather than entertainment.

16. Are your current actors specifically trained/experienced in TIE?

Many actors return to work with us and have developed their skills over time. However the main considerations are their skills both as performers and their respect towards children and young people.

17. Is training or experience in drama/TIE an employment criterion when making acting appointments?

No.

18. Are any of your actors teacher trained? Would this be an advantage?

No.

19. In what ways has TIE practice in your company changed or developed in recent years?

Work has gradually changed from co-devising to previously devised or commissioned work. This means an increase in production values and the security that the Company can be confident of the suitability of content before rehearsal period.

20. How confident are you about the future of TIE in Wales?

With the development of the *Strategy for Theatre in Education in Wales*, new money has been invested in the sector by the Assembly. This has given the companies the ability to plan long-term both financially and artistically. However, further investment is needed to fulfil the aims and objectives of the *Curriculum*.

21. How confident are you about the future of your company?

Due to the development of the *Strategy* the future of the Company is more secure than ever. Also, due to the introduction of the three year funding, contract investment is guaranteed for the next three years. The Company is also fortunate in the financial support it receives from the Local Authorities.

22. In percentage terms what are your sources of funding?

26% - Local Authority
74% - Arts Council of Wales.

23. Do you work in both primary and secondary schools? What is the percentage split between the two sectors?

10.5% of schools are secondary
89.5% of schools are primary

24. How many TIE projects does the company undertake each year?

Four. This number can vary. We sometimes get commissioned by various agencies to do additional projects.

25. Is your company also involved in community or other forms of theatre?

In the past we have been involved in drama workshops in the community and have received lottery funding to produce main stage productions. We have also run a Youth Theatre scheme.

26. Is your company involved in INSET training for teachers?

Yes. We provide a comprehensive INSET training day to coincide with each secondary school project. In the primary sector we arrange teacher workshops which usually last about 2 hours.

27. Do you have any further reflections on the current state of TIE in Wales?

There is a feeling that the eight companies are in a stronger situation to co-operate due to the new investment and through the development of the National Agency for Theatre in Education in Wales.

Name of Company: *Gwent TIE*   **Title of project:** *Home Front*
Date of Visit: 28/06/04   **Interviewee**: Gary Meredith   **Position:** Artistic Director
Interviewee: Jain Boon   **Position:** Director
Duration of Project: 90 mins [Performance 75 mins   Workshop 15 mins]

1. How would you define the Educational Aim of the project?

GM: One factor was that the children were studying the Second World War as part of their Curriculum. That was the starting point. When we started to look at ideas for material we decided that we didn't want just a history lesson. We wanted to look at children in unusual contexts and how that affected those individuals and their personal development. We wanted to underpin the historical perspective, but also to get children to look at and to question why we behave in the way that we do? And how we relate to each other. There was a strong element of personal and social education involved. To get us to question our behaviour and to ask why we are what we are.

JB: We didn't want it to be a piece about 'The War'. I think that the teachers can do that. There are things that can go into teachers' packs and that they can follow up later, but we wanted very much to focus on the human side of 'children being displaced'.

This was a re – tour. Did the project change much from the original?

GM: It was very similar. This was a new production with a new director, but the basic format was the same. It's not just a 're-tread' of the first production.

JB: And we were both involved in the original devising, so I had a strong sense of ownership and what the piece was about.

GM: We found it had new resonances because of world events and that was added into the equation – but I don't think it's changed to that extent. It's just about ordinary children in difficult and exceptional circumstances.

2. How was the project devised or developed?

JB: We read a lot of first-hand accounts of people's experiences during the war and some of that informed the educational content of the work. We started off by working with a writer, Philip Michell. And we talked to him, and he went off and did some research. He put together a pack for us to help us develop our research work. It's such a vast subject matter. He concentrated on the Blitz experience, women at war and, of course, the evacuation of children. With that we did our own bits of reading as well. At the time there were only three actors in the company, so that is why there were three main characters and the actors would all play the other characters in each one's stories. We wanted this idea of children being in a no-man's-land, a 'no-where-land' – but they needed to keep telling their story. Like a cycle – they would have to keep telling the story of their lives. We had great big discussions about whether these children were even alive! It started off as an extended improvisation. Phil sent us off to look at objects and the meaning of those objects to those children. We all went off and found certain things and then did a lot of role play and character-building. We looked at the emotional needs of the children – their emotional baggage as well as their actual baggage.

GM: We talked a lot about our own fears as children. We were not old enough to remember the war, but we used our own fears, and images of joy, sorrow, moments of parting. We took ideas from our own experiences that we had as children; parted from a parent perhaps for the first time, bereavement, loss of grandparents, something like that. We tried to inhabit the emotional life of the child as far as possible. The actors had a really strong sense of ownership with the eventual script. So much was generated through improvisation and discussion.

JB: I think our own personalities came through in terms of the scenes and the characters – they were very much bound up with the people that were first involved with the project.

3. How many performances of the project are planned?

GM: Oh… I don't know. It goes on for ever, doesn't it?!

JB: It's a long tour!

GM: In the region of 80. Tours have got longer because demand has increased.

4. Do you ever re-tour projects? Under what circumstances?

GM: One reason could be financial. Though that was not the case with this project. It was purely on the basis that it had had a very successful first outing. There was a very strong demand from schools asking if we had any plans to re-tour that project.

JB: We could probably do it every year, actually.

GM: It's really in response to schools whether we decide to re-tour.

JB: It also happens that this play is going to be published.

GM: It seemed to be a good time to re-tour it.

5. To what extent were teachers involved in the choice of material or the development of ideas?

GM: Yes, we do involve teachers. We take a questionnaire to schools when we tour a project and one of the questions is what areas or subject areas or issues they would like to see the company explore in future projects. That is where the original idea for this project came from. That consultation is almost token, but we also have a Teachers Advisory Panel and we also use other professionals when we need to. For example, we are working on a project about sexual health and social responsibility, so we've brought onto our panel sexual health workers as well as educationalists and other agencies. We do use this as a method to consult and, of course, we are talking to teachers all the time when we are touring. There's nothing like a cup of coffee in the staffroom to get responses and ideas.

6. Does the company attempt to identify the needs of the children when developing projects?

GM: As we said, we always try to look beyond the Curriculum requirements to what we think is important for children.

7. How would you describe your relationship with schools and what developments would you like to see?

GM: We do have a very good relationship with schools and a very good relationship with our advisory panel, but clearly there is a need to strengthen existing links and to create new ones with those schools that we have been less successful in engaging. To that end we have an Education Liaison Officer starting with us in September.

8. Do you employ a 'schools liaison' officer and what are the duties of this post?

GM: The role will very much concentrate on developments in education. It will enable us to consult much more widely with teachers than we are currently able to do about developments in education, what the teachers' needs are and what the needs of the children are. It will also involve promoting the work of the company in areas which haven't used our services as much as they might have done. They will also be involved in creating and making resource materials in consultation with ourselves as a team and where appropriate the advisory teachers. It's a fairly wide remit.

JB: I think that will also go some way to fill a gap that was left when the Authority broke up [Gwent now consists of five area Authorities]. Sometimes we are not able to get into schools that we need to get into quite as often as we would like. Some of the Authorities now have to pay for our services whereas we always used to have a free service for the whole area that we were serving. So we want to build contact with some of the schools that we've lost along the way.

GM: It's very complicated in that we used to only have one Authority to deal with and now we've got five. And they all have their own idiosyncratic ways of working. It must be said that there is a Director of Education Forum which we have access to, and I usually appear once a year and tell them what we are planning for the future. And we do get a good deal of cooperation and help both at a Director of Education level right down to the 'chalk face' or 'whiteboard' face.

9. Do you provide teaching materials/teaching packs and how are these compiled?

GM: The company has an input, but in recent years the Teachers' Advisory Service has taken a lead in preparing them. On the last couple of occasions we have actually employed someone to undertake the specific task of doing that. We found that with the Teachers Advisory Panel doing the pack, it wasn't being completed early enough. The teachers were saying more and more that they would really like the pack before the company went into the schools. The only way we could do that was to employ someone to pull it all together and to make sure that it was available at the teachers' preview. That has been very successful and very popular.

JB: Sammy Gibbins, who worked on the teachers' pack, was very much involved right from the beginning and we had consultations before the project started.

She came to rehearsals – she even came on a research day with us to the Imperial War Museum. Before we started actually looking at the script we did a lot of workshopping with our characters and what the play was about. She was very much involved in all that. She notated a lot of the sessions, drew pictures and took photos. She was very much involved in all of that. I think that one of the problems that we have found over the years is that Advisory Teachers have got such demands on their time that they couldn't always get packs out on time. They were just too busy to do those things.

GM: They tend to be rather detached from the process as well.

JB: There have been times when I have actually put the pack together.

GM: Use of the packs by teachers is patchy. This one is particularly interesting as two Authorities are using it as a 'transition' project [the project is being used in years 6 and 7 across junior and secondary to offer a continuity of experience as children move school], so in those schools the pack has been very well used. But it is patchy in other areas. Generally, with this one, most schools are using it well because it fits very neatly and tidily into the Curriculum. Some projects perhaps are not so clear as to where they are in terms of the National Curriculum.

JB: [to GM] Do you think the primary schools use them more than the secondary schools?

GM: I think that's probably right, yes. Often when we go back to primary schools we will see a whole body of work, artwork or written work, and we think, 'oh, that's the project we did last year'. You know, they've got a term's work out of it. And sometimes they send children's work in to us to see, which is really nice.

JB: With the 'transition project' the children have also been set tasks to do during the holidays, and the libraries have got involved as well. That's somebody else that's involved in the project. The idea is that people are actually following the children through and not just leaving them for the summer.

10. Does the project have identified links to Learning Objectives of the National Curriculum?

GM: This used to be quite vague, but we are now much keener to be able to identify the links, especially in secondary education. Teachers have to be able to justify the time, and other teachers need help to be able to identify where they can tick the boxes showing that they are covering the requirements of the National Curriculum. We are keen not to become – and I don't think we have – we don't want to be a sort of 'menu service' for the National Curriculum. We do work in schools and, therefore, there must be links with the National

Curriculum. In most projects it would be almost impossible not to find links. We do point out the links.

JB: We do. And we actually sit down and read the Curriculum!

GM: I recently spoke to SACRE about religious education. I read the RE Curriculum and you could look at just about anything and tick half the boxes. But I guess that teachers sometimes need to have it pointed out.

JB: Yes, I think so.

GM: There's still a tendency to think 'that's drama, that's English'. But our work can be applied across the curriculum. And that's what we want to do because we don't want to be thought of as the creatures that belong to the English or the Drama departments. That's an ongoing battle really.

11. Did the project include workshop or participatory elements? YES/NO

If yes, what governed the choice of methodologies?

JB: For me it depends on what age group the show is going to, what the subject matter is, and time. We did a project a while ago for secondary schools about domestic abuse, and we felt very strongly that we wouldn't just be able to go into a school and do a short discussion after opening up a can of worms. Fortunately, because of the age group it was going to – and it was funded directly by Newport Domestic Abuse Forum – it meant that we could spend a whole day in a school, and it meant we could do a pre-performance workshop, and then we did a participatory workshop in the afternoon. For me, it depends on time.

GM: If we had wanted to spend a whole day and use participatory methods we would have devised a different piece of work. When it was first devised, it was as essentially a performance piece with a shortish discussion and supported with a teachers' resource pack. You are really asking about day-long projects, and what we have found is that much of our work has become more performance-based than it would have been in years gone by. There are a number of reasons for that. One is that schools have become more reluctant to put aside a whole day for a project – because of changes in education and the demands on teachers. The other is the cost. We now have three Authorities which have to actually pay directly for the service. The other two fund directly so that it is free at the point of delivery. The other thing is that the demand for the work has become so great that we have had to find ways of reaching larger numbers of schools. Some might say that that has diluted the service. I hope that we have kept the integrity of the work, but obviously it has changed working practices. I do miss very much not being able to do the full-day programme, but I don't think it necessary that every programme is a full-day programme. I've never thought that, even in the 'good ol' days' when we could ring up and say, 'we'd like to come to your school tomorrow and work with year four all day' and they'd say, 'oh, great'. It really depends on the work. The project on domestic abuse clearly required a lot of detailed pre-work and follow-up work because we were in a situation where we were going to be faced with disclosure.

JB: And we were, quite often…

GM: We had to make sure that there was proper support there apart from the company to be able to deal with that. When we did the Bosnia project there were two workshops with that, but they didn't happen on the same day. This was to accommodate the secondary school timetable. We offered an initial workshop to examine the issues and we offered a theatre-based workshop which looked at theatre techniques. That was quite successful – but – what we did was ensure that the project would stand on its own with a short discussion and teacher pack. The workshops were optional extras that schools could use where they felt appropriate. So we've been experimenting…

JB: The key thing is, when we originally devised for this, we still had a 'host school' system. We would go to one school – say, the local comprehensive – and we would bring all the feeder schools in. Then we could afford to do projects of an hour twenty, an hour and a half in those days. Now we tend to do projects of about fifty minutes long so we've got time to talk. I think there's been quite a lot of pressure on the actors actually, because it is such a demanding piece emotionally anyway. The SM tends to lead the discussion sessions based on notes and questions which I have given him.

If no, why was the decision made not to use participatory elements?

12. Do you have a policy about the use of workshop and/or participatory work?

GM: It is a matter of pragmatism rather than anything else to be honest. I mean what we wouldn't do is deal with something like domestic abuse and not have a workshop. That wouldn't be responsible. We couldn't do a project like that and then have a twenty-minute chat after the show. Similarly with the sexual health project coming up – that will clearly need a workshop.

JB: At the moment we are talking about whether that will be a workshop after the production or whether, in fact, it might be with a team of two other people that might go in a day or a few days later, but…

GM: But the company will need to follow it up as well as teachers, with a teaching pack or something.

13. What theatrical influences currently affect your performance work?

JB: For me – I've just been to see a production by Shared Experience and I was completely bowled over. It is very physical and I felt very involved in it.

It was also quite a dark piece. I just remember coming out of that theatre and just thinking 'wow!' I want to see more of that kind of work. That was really exciting. I am also reading quite a lot about symbolism in the way we work – not just relying on the spoken word but finding other ways of communicating with the audience. With 'Home Front' I was especially looking for moments when I could do that, as one of the characters couldn't speak. Another thing is that people don't always tell the truth on stage – they might say something but feel something else. I spend quite a lot of time looking for moments like that, really, and how you might communicate those things and those feelings.

GM: I'm just a great 'nicker' of ideas. I've been quite inspired by some of Theatr Powys' recent work, which I thought was splendid. I'm also a great lover of the ballet, so, like Jain, I am interested in the physicality of the work, but I come at it from a different way. I do think visually, but I am a great believer in the spoken word as well. I like the 'storytellers' style – to use a broad term. So that could be Brechtian in nature. I like the very direct, unvarnished, relatively uncomplicated, quite stripped-down approach. And, seriously, I am influenced by the ballet – without actually having the dancing around!

JB: Shared Experience use a lot of German Expressionism, so, you know, when you say you are into ballet, movement and that sort of physicality, it's quite interesting to use different styles of physical work really.

Home Front was quite a challenging piece theatrically.

GM: We worried about that to start with. I mean, the play has been going on for five minutes and nobody's said anything yet.

JB: Gary has this imaginary friend called Flint. And he always says, 'I wonder what Flint will make of this?' But it was OK, Gary said, 'Flint will be fine, just give him some time!'

14. What drama influences currently affect your participatory work?

JB: We can't help being influenced by people like Gavin Bolton or Dorothy Heathcote. We may not be pure followers of their work, but, I am the next generation after you and Gary that have come into this work, so I've never seen them in action although I have read some books. What I have done is worked with people like Louise Osborn at Theatr Powys, and I think I have been quite influenced by *her*. As Bolton says, you take what you want…

GM: Absolutely.

JB: That's right. Things get adapted and handed down.

GM: When I see some Boal, I think, actually I was doing this thirty-five years ago. Sometimes you think you have invented something yourself, but it is usually out there somewhere. Also, when we have different directors, guest directors, they bring different ideas. In this way we have rediscovered Commedia Del Arte because a particular director liked to use Commedia Del Arte techniques.

15. What do you feel are the key differences between Theatre for Children and Theatre in Education?

JB: We do think there's a difference, but we think the waters have got muddied over the years. I know companies that are called Children's Theatre or Theatre for Children, and they do produce educational packs and talk to their children afterwards, but…

GM: *Tinder Box*. That was Children's Theatre. It toured to large audiences which you can't control. You can only recommend that it is suitable for a certain age range and then it's up to individual mums and dads. It's not having control of those things at a fairly basic level. Also, the way in which the piece was written and pitched in a way that could work reasonably satisfactorily for younger children and be quite satisfying for older children. A family show, if you like. With Theatre in Education you are more focussed on the age group we are playing to. So in devising, writing, commissioning – however it's arrived at – the piece will be targeting a fairly specific age group, and we would be identifying a number of educational aims, objectives that the piece should have – and…

JB: And we produce teachers' packs and employ somebody to go and run workshops in the local area that we were touring to.

GM: And I think we would expect that there were certain, if not learning, outcomes, that they could tick a box – there would be some sort of learning outcome, however that may be expressed. And with a piece of Children's Theatre I think that those things may still exist. Maybe it's just that those things are not be so well focussed. A few years ago we felt that Theatre in Education must have a participatory element to qualify as theatre in education and the debate that raged was 'is this drama in education or is it theatre in education?' I think that many, not all, but many, have become more… more performance-based. And I think that the quality of performance has improved. I am not commenting on our own company. That is for other people to judge, not me – but I think the quality of performance work has just, well… I mentioned *Theatr Powys* earlier, and I thought "*South of Solitude*" was a splendid piece, though I haven't seen it with its whole workshop. I thought the quality of performance in that piece was really, really high quality.

16. Are your current actors specifically trained/experienced in TIE?

JB: One of them, Dora Jones, has been working in Theatre in Education for years. But trained? Trained as in 'trained on the job', rather than doing a specific course. She is hugely experienced and so feels very comfortable about workshopping the children and talking to the kids.

17. Is training or experience in drama/TIE an employment criterion when making acting appointments?

GM: It should be a consideration, but I wouldn't say it is an essential criterion, because I wouldn't want to rule out of the equation someone who is really good at working with children or who wants to work with children. We would always look for someone who was genuinely interested rather than someone who thinks of it as 'just another job'. You can never be absolutely certain.

JB: It does make a difference though.

GM: It does. A person's attitude. It does communicate. When you meet people at interview and you workshop them, interview them and what have you… I really wouldn't want a team of actors on the road where none of them had had that experience, all rookies, if you like. The other skills can be learned on the job, and that is something that I know a lot of us are very conscious of. As for the rising generation? A lot more actors are freelance, zipping from one thing to another. What we are trying to get back to as a company is to establish more of a core company, so that you keep a body of experience together. Then, when you do have somebody who's new to the work, maybe a recent graduate or even a local person, they will be coming into a family of people with skills and into a situation where those skills can be shared.

JB: It is very time consuming to be training new actors for each project. Gary and I have been working together for about thirteen years so we have got a sort of shorthand in our work. So on one hand you do want to give time and energy to someone new coming in, but if you had to do it all the time it would slow up the process, I guess.

18. Are any of your actors teacher trained? Would this be an advantage?

JB: They're all actor trained.

GM: Yes. There's no one really who's teacher trained.

JB: It would be another skill and it would be an advantage. It certainly wouldn't be a necessity.

GM: I don't think the role is the same as a teacher. I know there are elements of being a teacher – running a workshop and so on. It's a bit different from being a teacher. And those skills can, can be learned. I mean, you wouldn't put somebody in a workshop on his or her own. You'd put them alongside someone with more experience, which we have done. Most actors quickly pick up the skills and confidence that they need.

19. In what ways has TIE practice in your company changed or developed in recent years?

JB: I think that TIE practise has changed, and one reason is the times that we live in, and the society and the political changes that have happened. I think that informed the work. I read recently a trilogy of plays that had been produced by Belgrade and M6 and had actually seen a piece of that work that influenced me in such a way that I wanted to work in Theatre in Education. But having looked at it recently, I found some of it quite naïve and unsophisticated now. It certainly wouldn't have been at the time, and I think it was to do with the time it was written, the methodology and the practices that were in use at the time.

GM: I think that a lot of the work has got a kind of theatrical literacy which was not always apparent in some of the earlier work. That is not to say that it was absent from earlier work. There was some great work done in those earlier days. Some fantastic work.

JB: [to GM] You put it very well the other day. You said it was to do with the information that we used to put into our plays. At one time we felt the need to do the teacher's job and the resource pack job and everything – that was one of the things you were saying…

GM: It wasn't true of all projects. I can think of a lot of pieces that were like that… I can put my hand up as guilty. Those pieces which were just full of information – shoving all the research and all the information in there. I think, well, just think of the Theatr Powys' piece. What a piece of sharp, sophisticated, beautifully observed and performed piece of theatre. And I don't see the quality of performance in the early stuff – and I know that's a generalization. I'm not saying we were bad actors thirty years ago…

JB: It came out of, what was it, agitprop?…

GM: I think there was an element of that. I think there was a kind of 'cause'. I think the politics, (Theatr Powys wouldn't agree with this, of course) I think that the kind of radical left-wing agenda has all but disappeared for the most part. I think that has changed the approach and attitude to a lot of the work. I suppose that some people would say it's become flabby, liberal, social democrat…

20. How confident are you about the future of TIE in Wales?

GM: When I look around and see the work of other companies, I feel greatly heartened. It is changing and it will continue to change. In another ten years it may be a completely different beast again, I don't know. But I'm confident that there are good things happening.

JB: And there seems to be a real, you know… the Assembly is putting more money into companies, and the Arts Council, the Education Authorities. The companies are all talking to each other again and trying to find a way forward. I find that very heartening.

GM: And what is interesting as well is that the companies are diverse. There isn't a 'party line' or single agenda. Companies are quite different in a number of ways; that, I think, is excellent. If the political will remains, I am very confident about the future of TIE in Wales.

21. How confident are you about the future of your company?

GM: Yes, I like to think that the company will be around for many years to come. In terms of the relationship we have with schools and other organizations, in terms of the strong, very active Board, and in terms of the management structure of the company, in terms of its finance, I think the company is well placed to continue, I mean, if Jain and I walked under a bus tomorrow the company would continue. It's not a one-woman/one-man outfit, you know, it's a company.

22. In percentage terms what are your sources of funding?

GM: The vast majority is ACW. About 80 per cent.

JB: Then there's the funding from Blaenau Gwent and Monmouthshire.

GM: For the other three Authorities, what we do is charge so much per head. Technically, it should be about £250 per performance. That's a hundred children.

JB: But occasionally some of the Authorities will say, 'we recognize the importance of this project and we'll put that much money into that production' which may halve what the schools have to pay or sometimes enable us to offer it free.

GM: We get funny deals like… Newport, for example, they withheld funds but then they bought a package, the Local Authority bought a package of twelve performances to go into all their secondary schools. So the schools didn't have to pay anything – the authority found extra money. Caerphilly does similar things or has done in the past. But obviously that's for projects that are 'flavour of the month'. In total it's about 80 per cent from the Arts Council and 20 per cent from the Authorities. Other income is very small, but we've got to charge something or else the authorities that are funding us say, 'well, why are *we* funding you?'

23. Do you work in both primary and secondary schools? What is the percentage split between the two sectors?

GM: Setting up and preparation time is about the same whether it's primary or secondary. The length of tours is shorter in secondary by virtue of the fact that there are fewer schools. We usually do a seven-week tour for secondary schools, and primary tours go on for ever!

JB: Some primary schools have a very short afternoon, so you can only do one a day.

GM: Some only do an hour after lunch! One hour! It's not worth going back after lunch.

24. How many TIE projects does the company undertake each year?

GM: We have been doing three tours a year: infant, junior and secondary. Occasionally, there might be an additional project with additional funding – like the domestic abuse project. From now on, we will be doing four a year because we are reinstating Welsh-language projects

25. Is your company also involved in community or other forms of theatre?

GM: We run a youth theatre. There is a Monday group for disadvantaged children. They get referred to us.

JB: There is a Tuesday group with about forty in it and forty more on the waiting list!

GM: Then there are Saturday sessions…

JB: And, because we've got a studio here, we have visiting companies. We did used to do community touring, but we can't afford to do that. We think there should be extra money put into that. But we do give performances of our TIE work occasionally in the community.

GM: We nearly always do a couple of performances of the TIE work. There are very few projects that we wouldn't do that with. And that is basically an unashamedly public relations exercise. But it is also a genuine attempt and opportunity to encourage members of the general public to see the work.

26. Is your company involved in INSET training for teachers?

GM: At least a couple of times a year. I did one with Charlie Way recently…

JB: I did a Shakespeare workshop

GM: Actually in the last couple of years it's about six.

JB: And we've got one coming up with Louise about this sexuality project. That's working with teachers as a trailer for the project we are going to be doing.

27. Do you have any further reflections on the current state of TIE in Wales?

GM: It was very interesting at the TIE conference recently when what became clear is that there is a disagreement about what constitutes theatre in education and quite what the work should be. There's nothing new in that. You will remember years ago when there were very bitter arguments raging over it. But what was a good development was the fact that, after all the pain that people have been through in recent years, that people are beginning to talk to each other again. There are good developments in the work and positive feelings. I recently saw some English companies performing – not exactly TIE – but there was nothing that Wales can't match.

JB: TIE is as important now as ever. To introduce young people to theatre and to understand its importance and educationally to get them to express opinions and develop values. The need for TIE will never go away. How we do it might change, but the need for what it can do will always be there.

Name of Company: *Theatr Iolo* **Title of project:** *Journey*
Date: 1/07/04 **Interviewee**: Kevin Lewis **Position:** Director
Duration of Project: 45 minutes [Performance 45 Workshop 0]

1. How would you define the Educational Aim of the project?

Phew! The educational aim of the project? I'm not sure that we would start from an educational aim. We would start from an artistic aim. This project was created about ten years ago when we had the luxury of quite a lot of funding and we decided we wanted to do a project that we didn't know what it was going to be until it 'was'. We wanted to work from an artistic stimulus and there were some strong performers in the company and we wanted to experiment really; to see what we could create. One of the actors in the company was interested in the work of Picasso. We took his work as a starting point – I mean, we were all interested in visual things, design ideas. We experimented with these ideas and gradually a play appeared. And elements started to come out which were educational. We knew we were going to do it for four- to seven-year-olds – that was the age group that traditionally we did at that time of the year. One can be quite open with what one does with that age group. So we experimented with all these ideas and, in the end, the play is about two people who start off by not cooperating and by the end of the play they have worked it through. On a feeling level it was a play which was exploring notions of feeling, friendship, things like that. From a 'Picasso' point of view, which is maybe more interesting, the design had a playful element in it with lots of the objects in the play being used in different ways. The set is basically a lot of junk, what Picasso might use – boxes, bits of wood, and they are made into different ramifications to create the environment. Our desire was very much to create a visual piece of theatre; that interested us. When we started doing it in schools they got a lot out of it. So in a sense, the education came afterwards. We created a play – a play that we wanted to do, but at the back of our minds we knew that we were working on a play for four- to seven-year-olds. When we created the storylines we were quite interested in Shakespearean plots, so it starts off quite domestically but then you get into devices which make it quite epic. There is someone who is mistaken for being dead, they are taken off to sea, there's a storm, they see a ghost – lots of coincidences. They end up on a desert island and they have to survive, there's a bird that talks… The education sort of came afterwards. We thought 'what could a group of children in an infant school get from this play?' and in the resource pack that we have developed for this tour we took various themes like 'what can I see?' There is a whole section on seeing and looking. Lots of exercises about how an artist 'looks'. There is stuff in there about storytelling, making up stories, creating narrative. There is a section in the pack which is to do with emotion – looking at the play and working out what different emotions different people are feeling at different times and why they might feel those emotions. And looking at what was going on in the play – the human questions and the characters' motives: Why do they feel threatened? Why don't they want to make friends? Why won't they share? There are bits of behaviour which are totally relevant to the age group.

2. How was the project devised or developed?

Well, as I have mentioned, we started with the Picasso stimulus, worked on it as a company and we ended up with a script that came from the devising process.

Not using a writer?

No, not using a writer. It came from the actors. And two of the original cast have a great deal of devising experience and that fed into it. In fact, there's not a huge amount of written text. There's a lot of non-verbal stuff in it. This is a project that we have done three or four times.

3. How many performances of the project are planned?

About forty in this current tour, but there will be over a hundred performances in all this year.

4. Do you ever re-tour projects? Under what circumstances?

As I said, this has been often re-toured. We have been going to Europe quite a bit and getting to know companies there. One of the things that they do is to keep work in repertoire. It struck me that what we tend to do in Britain is to create things and then we go onto the next. We're constantly creating new things. In the end we decided that there was actually a lot of good stuff in our 'back catalogue', and some of it is worth revisiting and this actually eases the pressure. And what it actually does (and this ties up with work I've been doing in the Welsh College with young training actors) is that by taking a piece that is already devised and created, or by taking scripted pieces, it is quite interesting – because you can then in the rehearsal process *not* spend all the time devising something. You can concentrate on some of the other things which *sometimes* in a devising process can get missed out because you are all the time creating the work. Those are the reasons why we do it. The criterion for re-touring is pieces that we like and that are good – and also pieces which have gone down well. We'd be stupid to revive pieces that we really like but, in fact, nobody wants. But it isn't just essentially about 'oh, this will sell.' Essentially it is about 'is it good for us?' In this particular instance there are other reasons. We started last year doing some interesting work for under-fives, three- to five-year-olds. A show called *Are We There Yet?* which we performed in nurseries for groups of about twenty kids. Economically it wasn't worthwhile, but in an artistic sense it was. The schools were crying out for stuff like that. We've had fantastic success taking it to venues in England, and we've just been to a festival in Belgium and performed it in French. Because this term has been very busy doing that, and we've been doing a show for secondary schools which got invited to a festival in Scotland, we had to find something that we could put together quite quickly. This time it only had a three-day rehearsal period. Two of the cast had been in it before and we got a new person in. So, in one sense, there have been some pragmatic reasons for this re-tour.

5. To what extent were teachers involved in the choice of material or the development of ideas?

Apart from the fact that there are teachers on our Board and that we have an Education Office, we also have a lot of contact with teachers and we are talking to teachers all the time. In the sense of asking teachers specifically what they want, well… we are really artistically driven in a sense, and we are more at the 'Film Four' artistic end rather than doing things about refugees and World War Two because that happens to be the big syllabus thing. My question to companies like that would be whether they themselves are actually interested in that. Or are they just doing that because that is what the Curriculum wants? We have been down that road in the past – you know, really looking at the Curriculum and slavishly following what is required.

6. Does the company attempt to identify the needs of the children when developing projects?

No. It's terrible, isn't it?! No, really, I don't anymore. Except that I think that children should be exposed to really good material and really good theatre. And good stories. And obviously it has got to make some connection with them somewhere. To give a case in point, a few years ago I saw a play performed by a Dutch company, in English, about three brothers left in the house by their father. The whole play is a speculation about what is happening to the family: is the dad coming back? It all becomes a bit 'Lord of the Flies' – it's a really powerful play about these boys' fear of abandonment, sibling rivalry, all sorts going on in this 'hothouse'. I saw this play and this group of Norwegian teenagers enwrapped in it. Then they act out what they imagine their father is doing; they take on the role of the father. It's an exploration of masculinity and fatherhood. It's a fantastic play and I thought, 'I want to do this, this is great'. I thought anyone could get things out of this, particularly teenagers; there is a lot in there for teenagers. To come back to the question, okay, we are artistically driven, but a couple of years ago we did a thing about divorce and stepchildren. It started with the things that I said to the writer about – 'what's it like if you are ten years old and you suddenly get a brother or sister of the same age as you living in your house?' I was interested in this personally, and it is pretty clear that lots of other children are going through that. It's a mixture of the two, but I do think that if I am not interested in it, then it's not going to work. And as a company we are trying to find things which are not just narrowly about one thing. We are trying to find things which are rich and could be about a whole range of things. And in some of the workshops we've done, when we have done workshops with shows, you know, different things come out depending on the interests of the group; they might speculate about different things.

7. How would you describe your relationship with schools and what developments would you like to see?

I think our relationship is pretty good to a certain extent. It could be improved in that we could get more schools on board. I realize that in a sense we have set ourselves a difficult task. In some cases we have chosen to do 'challenging' things – things that are slightly different. When you say to schools, 'oh, this is a Dutch play', they're actually not interested if it is from Holland. But if you said, 'we're doing *Under Milk Wood* and that's on the syllabus', they'd be more interested. So some of the things have not sold as easily as we might like. We still have to charge schools. It's cut down to about £1 a head and we limit the audiences. It tends to be the same schools who book, and that's what I mean by 'getting more schools on board'. We have been able to offer some free performances when we have had extra bits of subsidy. I would like to go back to the free services because it's just a bloody pain trying to sell things. The great thing about selling projects is that we have had a lot of exposure at venues and festivals and other places that want us, but that's not necessarily the idea. That's great for the actors and the company – to go off to Edinburgh, or wherever, and get reviews, and it's important that things like that happen, but one of the things that we are working on is how we get more schools on our side. I'm sure that every company has similar targets to get to more schools, and part of the problem is that teachers are very busy: secondary schools are a bloody nightmare. It takes a lot of effort to organize, to get the kids off timetable. Just before Christmas a Head of Drama wanted to book a particular show and she had to take it to her Senior Management Committee. She came back and said she 'couldn't have it because they had already had something else this term and the head doesn't want people to go 'off Curriculum' – but if you come back in July when we have an arts week…'. You know, we're not touring it then. So we are starting to think about making it a bit easier for secondary schools and actually thinking about doing plays which can actually take place in a classroom. For example, there is a Danish play we might do, a two-hander which can easily take place in a classroom with no set whatsoever. It requires really good acting. It's about a gang of girls basically. One of them is dead and one of them is alive. Between them they enact and tell the story of this group of girls. Just in a practical sense, the idea of just going into a classroom and being able to play to a group of 30 kids and perform it in the classroom and use the desks and what's there is very attractive. Apparently that's happening quite a lot in Europe. There was this really interesting play I heard about where the 'teacher' comes into the classroom, so the audience are like the young people in the class and proceeds to start teaching a lesson, doing the things that teachers do, walking up the aisle, sitting on the desk. Then it starts to break down and it turns out the play is about teenage suicide. A boy in his class has killed himself, and he's getting the blame and it's quite a big subject matter. But I'm just really interested in the format. In a way it goes back to some of those old TIE things, when you go into a classroom and give them things to do. So secondary schools are really hard to access. We did a Charlie Way play last year – it ran about an hour and ten minutes – and if the kids arrived late [which they sometimes did] then you run up against all those things… We ended up by doing it to smaller groups in drama studios – it just seemed to be a lot better than having massive great audiences.

8. Do you employ a 'schools liaison' officer and what are the duties of this post?

We have an Education Officer. One thing they have to do is, with the company, to create the resource pack. Another thing is to do the pre-workshops if that is what we are doing. Or post-workshops. Again, we have stopped offering workshops to every school. It's just not possible to do that. As a company we've become more performance-based. Trying to fit workshops within the timetable didn't really work and so what we've done is that with some projects we offer workshops. Some projects don't have workshops with them at all and other projects have workshops if the schools want to buy them in. The Education Officer would do things like that. At other times she will initiate projects. I suppose that in a way she will work in schools in whatever way seems appropriate. She does a lot of work in schools that the company doesn't actually do a lot of work with in order to then get them to buy a performance. She's also been doing some research into a special needs project because that's her specialism. We are trying to raise some funds for it, and we are looking towards creating a project for severely autistic children which would involve a music therapist, a visual artist and a performance, which will be working with one child at a time. So it's highly labour intensive. And done over a period of time as well.

9. Do you provide teaching materials/teaching packs and how are these compiled?

I went to a seminar organized by ASSITEJ,* which was about imaginative resource materials, and this guy from Nottingham had done something for a company up North which involved the schools being given a rucksack, and within the rucksack were various objects – it was a show for special schools – so it was a sort of 'sensory work pack'. That was really interesting as a concept, so what we've tried to do in the last few years is to create resource material that in some way artistically reflects the show. For example, in the Picasso show we give the schools a picture that Picasso did painted on newspaper and then there are various work cards and suggestions. With the under-five show a teapot featured in the show so we gave the school a teapot wrapped up. Again there was stuff inside – we had Grimms' tales, there was sort of 'story string' and there were objects related to the story which could also be used to create other stories. We've worked very hard to write very succinct work packs so there's not necessarily a lot of stuff in them. In fact, there is so much resource material around for teachers that you don't want to overburden them. In a way it's better to find six or seven really good ideas that are succinct and they might pick up one or two. The other thing that we think is important with our resource material is to give some quite detailed synopsis of the play – a scene-by-scene breakdown so that, actually, they've got something to use as a starting point.

10. Does the project have identified links to Learning Objectives of the National Curriculum?

No. We used to do that, but in the end we thought 'actually they know all that'. We had these packs which contained all that and, actually, you are teaching your grandmother to suck eggs. In some ways we've gone the opposite way to some companies. We've stopped calling ourselves 'Theatre in Education'. We stopped calling ourselves that. We then started calling ourselves 'theatre for young people' and now we just call ourselves Theatr Iolo. For a variety of reasons. It wasn't that I wasn't proud of what we were doing, but it was just that it seemed to be this term of abuse in some quarters. I mean, you go to Europe and they say, 'oh, god, the stuff in Britain is all educational and worthy'. I suppose in the end it's a mixture of stuff. What I'm saying is that we are a theatre company. We produce plays. In the same way that a children's writer doesn't get asked by their publisher 'what are the aims of this book?' They just start to write it and create the piece that they want to create. Then people will take from it what they will. I always wanted to be in an experimental theatre company, basically, and I went to Teacher Training College, and I like young people and I ended up working for a young people's theatre in education company. I actually realized that you could be very experimental in those companies *and* you can have an audience! I became very interested in that interaction with the audience; there being some sort of meeting ground. This whole question of 'what is the worth of a piece of theatre' is one that one constantly struggles with, I think. I went through a period of doing historical pieces and quite enjoyed that because every project is an opportunity to learn about something. But in the end you think, 'well, I've done things on the Second World War and on drugs and that was interesting, but I don't actually want to do that for myself again. You sometimes get into that thing with the schools when they say: 'oh, could you do that thing on alcohol again'… Yeah. At times other director's have come in and done those things but in the end you have to follow your own interests and try and create an identity for yourself as a company. I think that's one of the things that we try to do. I think that we fell into a trap when we lost our funding in1992 – until about '95, '96 – of trying to be everything to everyone. We said 'yes' to everything. And now we think 'we don't have to say "yes" to everything. Let's do what we want.' One of the things we have started to do is translations of good plays – one of our 'aims' is to bring the best of world theatre to Cardiff and the Vale. We've done a Dutch play, we did a version of some Grimms' tales. We feel very much that we are a European company. Though based in Cardiff, we have been very lucky to go to festivals, do workshops with other companies, and I think our aim would be to do some sort of co-production with a company from Europe with actors from different nationalities who perform in different companies. That sort of cultural exchange is really interesting.

11. Did the project include workshop or participatory elements? YES/NO

If yes, what governed the choice of methodologies?

If no, why was the decision made not to use participatory elements?

Other than what I have already said, part of the reason is that we haven't had the actors with the skills to do that because we have been operating on short-term contracts. Part of it has been to do with the financial reason that we, having lost our funding, had to become more performance-orientated. We needed to bring in income. We had to start performing shows for audiences of a hundred.

12. Do you have a policy about the use of workshop and/or participatory work?

No. At some point I just got fed up with struggling with workshops and started to think I just want to start concentrating on the play; letting the play speak for itself and doing the resource material. For a particular project we might. I think we got into a trap of thinking that because we had always done workshops because the schools kept asking for workshops and then you've got sixty kids in there and it all became a bit meaningless. But where we have managed to create a good situation – for example, in a special school, or working with a GCSE drama group, or a smallish group, and we have the skilled performers – then workshop will go better. It certainly started to become a bit of a bind, doing the workshops. But having said that, a theatre company is ever changing. One of the things that we have been talking about is using the schools as more of a resource for the company to test out material with before we do it, so in the autumn we are doing a piece based on the folk tales of some of the new countries in the EU. Polish and Czech tales. We've found this tale which is a version of *King Lear*, and we've been to four schools, just taking bits of that story, acting sections out and asking them about it. I've been reading them extracts from the story and finding out if there are any bits of the story which relate to them. That's been a sort of prototype, and we've had some fantastic conversations about 'lying' and 'how do you know who loves you the most?', 'what sort of advice would you give someone faced with that question?' But in a way we can't possibly – well, we could if we wanted, but I don't particularly want to do that – do that with every single school group. But the idea of using that sort of participatory thing as a way of researching the material and helping us create the piece of theatre is artistically very appealing.

13. What theatrical influences currently affect your performance work?

Beyond what I have already said, it's things like *Theatre de Complicité*, and the work I've seen in Europe has that 'Jacques le Coq' feel about it. Going back a bit further, there's Peter Brook and the use of simplicity in the storytelling. For me, that sort of imaginative theatre… 'poor theatre', in a sense. It's about that simplicity and using everyday objects and transforming them. Another thing which concerns me is to do with the work I am doing at the Welsh College which is about the importance of eye contact and truthfulness in acting. Trying to really work on the acting of the company. At the heart of our work it is about good acting and good actors. The relationship between those actors and between them and the audience. I'm not interested in technology – we light our shows and we use a lot of composed music and ambient sound.

14. What drama influences currently affect your participatory work?

Well, I buy various drama books and you constantly come back to people like Dorothy Heathcote, but I don't know so much about that stuff now. We have contact with drama teachers in the county and we go on the courses they organize, and they have people like Neelands and people like that. But it's not something I've kept up with as much as the theatre side of things.

15. What do you feel are the key differences between Theatre for Children and Theatre in Education?

The big thing for me is to do with definitions. A lot of companies describe themselves as 'theatre in education companies' – you've only got to read the Stage. I would say that Theatr Powys is a classic theatre in education company – working with small groups, participatory, all-day programmes. To me that's Theatre in Education in the purest sense. Companies that do a play with a twenty-minute workshop at the end and nothing much of any depth happens in it doesn't seem particularly like theatre in education. I don't understand why people want to call it that – perhaps it gives them credibility or whatever. There *is* a difference and that's probably it. But theatre for young people – and I hope this is true for me and our company – can have an intelligence and significance or meaning. I have mixed feelings about the 'theatre in education' term. It's become a bit tarnished. That's not to say it's not valuable as a term. I actually think that it is not a term for us; we don't actually do that. We are not actually a Theatre in Education company here. Okay, we might say 'yes' to the National Assembly, but we're not there to try and help their social inclusion agenda. We're a theatre company. Our purpose is to create theatre. We can then make it accessible and help people into it.

16. Are your current actors specifically trained/experienced in TIE?

They've come from a variety of backgrounds. Most of them have come from the Welsh College. Well, Emyr [John] has been with the company for some time. He has been on a course at the Sherman for workshop leaders based on the work of Chris Johnston. So he has quite a lot of skills which will develop.

17. Is training or experience in drama/TIE an employment criterion when making acting appointments?

No. My criterion is getting someone who's a good performer.

18. Are any of your actors teacher trained? Would this be an advantage?

My experience has been that when we have had teachers applying for things here they have not actually been very good performers. I trained as a teacher, so maybe I'm not very good either!! There are some teachers who are good performers. I don't know. It certainly wouldn't *stop* me seeing somebody – we'll see anybody who sounds interesting. But, ostensibly, I'm looking for people who can act. And in a way, by employing an Education Officer, and by myself going out and doing some of the educational stuff, we've sort of separated the two things off.

19. In what ways has TIE practice in your company changed or developed in recent years?

We regard ourselves less and less as a TIE company and more as a theatre company that goes into schools and from which teachers can extract educational value. I find it quite useful to think in terms of literature. I was saying to a group of English teachers the other day that we are proposing to do this Danish piece... 'no, it's not on the syllabus' and 'yes, there are companies that will do that', 'it's not about a particular issue like alcoholism or whatever – it's about a range of things. It's like a short story; a good short story and surely as an English teacher you still have space in the curriculum... I've read this short story at the weekend, the kids will really respond to this, let's bring it in and let's read it.' In the world we're in now some people will do a lot of work around it and some will just watch the play and that's it. In a way though, to me, that's enough. It's fine just to watch the play. Another thing we have been doing in secondary schools is to offer workshops which are not particularly about the play but rather how we created the play and how we put a piece of theatre together.

Which actually ties in more to the Curriculum?

Well, it does. Absolutely. They have to write reviews on plays and in a way it's a sort of selling thing and I don't have any problem with doing that. In fact, I quite enjoy doing those workshops because you do start talking about what the play is about. It's a different emphasis doing workshops that are about theatrical techniques that we might have used. In the end our educational aims are educational in the widest sense of the word. The company just wants to bring good theatre to the children in whatever forms that might take, and that will in a way reflect their lives and the lives of other people.

20. How confident are you about the future of TIE in Wales?

I think the funding level is very good now. All the companies have had their funding pretty much doubled. When I am speaking to colleagues in England they are like 'f*cking hell!' It is a hell of a lot of money. Whether it will last and whether it will get sustained or not is another matter.

21. How confident are you about the future of your company?

Pretty confident. We've always been a company to go down interesting routes. Losing our funding [in 1992] was quite a good thing because it did actually sharpen us up and make us think about things in a different way. That's where the whole repertoire thing started to come from. This last couple of years there's been a lot of just practical things to consider about how you keep things in repertoire: things like storage, getting actors back, how much time do you need to rehearse somebody else in if you can't get the original cast. If you accept a festival date two years down the line, how do you guarantee you are going to get the same cast – all those things. How do you do three or four shows in tandem – and that's quite interesting. It's the way that one has to work. I'm feeling quite confident and, being quite candid here, you look at the range of what companies are doing in Wales and it's like in any country. It's a sort of mishmash of stuff, and I don't think that anyone has really got to the bottom of what you do if a company's work is not really that good. Some of the young actors in Welsh College are quite critical of the work that they see the companies doing, 'bloody hell, I wouldn't want to do that sort of theatre'. That needs to be dealt with. I think it's the case that the companies are actually talking to each other but they are all very different. There are some strong characters around and there are some interesting disagreements, arguments and things which can be fruitful. I think the strongest thing is the variety. I think that's good. It's good that we're all different in a way. And one of the things that I am very passionate about is about not just staying in Cardiff. I'd like to take our work to other parts of Wales, to Theatr Clwyd where they bring people in. And similarly we are very interested in bringing other companies into our area. If schools have a wider range of choice it can't be a bad thing. One of the interesting things with this new money coming in was that we could actually programme work, like a rep might do with other things coming in. We did a little bit of that last year. We brought in a puppet company from Norwich with whom we arranged a Welsh performance using a storytelling narration alongside it. We've got other plans to bring in another company to bring them into schools for a week here. We'd like to set up a small festival and bring in three or four companies, programme them into the schools and provide the educational activities that might be necessary to go alongside these events. So, to me, that's all quite new and quite exciting.

22. In percentage terms what are your sources of funding?

We get most money from the Arts Council. Cardiff provides the building and there is also some money at the whim of the council. We also raise box office from schools, but mainly from festivals and venues. The figures are about 80 per cent ACW, 15 per cent Box office and 5 per cent Cardiff.

23. Do you work in both primary and secondary schools? What is the percentage split between the two sectors?

It's mainly primary schools. There are only thirty-five secondary schools. That's another thing. We've started to do fewer projects but do them for longer.

24. How many TIE projects does the company undertake each year?

We tend to do a show for infants, a show for juniors and a show for secondary – Key Stage Three usually. That's not to say we wouldn't do Key Stage Four, but that would tie us more to the Curriculum. In a sense the interesting area has been the early years stuff – that's a whole new area and we've met some really interesting companies in Europe working with two-year-olds. There was a company that we met in Belgium that were doing some Garcia Lorca with an opera singer for two-year-olds and it was fantastic. I heard about this dance that was done with babies, and the dance was just copying the movements of the babies. That early years stuff has been quite an interesting area. An outside director came in to do that. We are doing some research and development for another project in December and that will go out next summer. That's been phenomenally successful. We went to Finland with it and Belgium.

25. Is your company also involved in community or other forms of theatre?

We haven't done that, no. We've done some family performances but we've not created a community show. It's not part of the company's brief. My big passion is that the work we do is designed for a particular age group but that when adults come to see it they think, 'wow, this is fantastic, this is good, if not better, than the other stuff'. For example, the play we did about the three brothers – if we did that again (and we probably will) – then one of the things I would really be interested in would be doing it for all-male audiences – like fathers and sons, brothers – free tickets if you come with your brothers! When we did it in Glasgow recently we had this e-mail from this dad with a fourteen-year-old son saying that they had had a fantastic time and that they had spent ages talking about it afterwards. I know that some theatres are quite interested in family audiences and, to me, that could be quite an interesting development – encouraging ways of getting parents, in this particular case a father-son thing, to experience theatre together. We've got a small youth theatre. Some girls came to us from a local secondary school wanting to start one up as part of some millennium volunteer scheme. We mentored them and helped them and got some funding for them. They did a production and with the funding we were able to bring in a director and designer. They took the production to their local primary schools, a Noel Greig play that Theatre Centre had done. On the strength of that, Cardiff asked us if Theatr Iolo could do a piece encouraging young people to vote – this whole 'people and democracy' thing. However, we sent them on their way because of the timing and because it was to be performed at this youth conference for about three hundred young people. But our small youth theatre – seven girls – they did it. They created it, they gave us money and we got this director to do it. On the strength of that, Cardiff gave us some money to do some skills workshops. So it's at the very early stages of developing into a youth theatre. It is something we'd like to do. I might on the one hand say I'm doing it because this is what I am interested in blah, blah, blah… but it's not as simple as that. We have an interest in young people, so by actually meeting young people and talking to young people you get a sort of inkling of what they are interested in. That's part of teaching, isn't it? Part of being a teacher is thinking, 'what ought I to be teaching my children?' You can just follow the Curriculum and, okay, that is what most people have to do. But if you are really serious about it, you are always asking yourself the question, 'what's it good for?' and 'what's the important thing to do now?' 'What should we talk about today?' When it comes down to it I don't think that children are any different to adults apart from their age and experience – there's still a lot of the same things going on. So in a sense what's in the air and what's in the world determines what theatre we should make now – what's the important story to tell now? It's sort of in the air, isn't it? And you sort of sniff these things out. There was a time last year when lots of people were doing things about war – that was a concern of people. We were thinking, well, actually there's a lot of that about so we'll do something different. We did this Charlie Way play but it was more about the war in people's hearts. And, you know, sometimes you react against things. The Europe thing came about because I suppose we had done Grimms' and, I suppose, in a way, at the back of our heads, there was a sort of feeling that some of us had been talking about. We have this sort of fantasy. If we were running a course on young people or children's theatre, the repertoire would include Grimms', the Greeks, Eastern Europe…

26. Is your company involved in INSET training for teachers?

Yes. Usually this is related to the project or during the creation of a project. This is good in some ways, but in other ways they tend to think it can be done in a day. We are never sure if there is any follow-up, but we are keen to make sure that the teachers feel part of it. Sometimes we are invited by companies and sometimes by the county. I'm not sure that the teachers take much away with them that they can use, but they really enjoy just *doing* it. They are getting a great deal out of it but I don't know how much they actually take back to schools.

27. Do you have any further reflections on the current state of TIE in Wales?

I think that there will be a crisis in a few years' time because of the fact that the directors are aging! We need new blood, new directors, especially women. In Wales it is a very male-dominated scene. It's starting to feel like a closed shop. Who is going to take over? Where will the new blood come from? Plenty of people can direct shows, but today they also need to be able to run companies. Perhaps it needs a new ACW trainee directors scheme – or maybe companies need to find money from current funding. Another issue that I feel strongly about is that some companies need to look beyond Wales and see what is happening in Britain and the world. There is insularity in some quarters. I feel it is important for companies to be part of ASSITEJ – to go to festivals and recharge the batteries – to meet people doing the same thing as you but doing it differently.

*The *Association International du Theatre pour l'Enfance et la Jeunesse /International Association of Theatre for Children and Young People* is an international networking organization promoting Theatre for Young People with centres in over ninety countries.

Name of Company: *Theatr Na n'Og*   **Title of project:** *Big Bad Wolf*
Date of Visit: 30/06/04 **Interviewee:** Rachel Clancy **Position:** Education Officer
Additional responses: *Geinor Jones* **Position:** Director
Duration of Project: 50 mins [Performance 45   Workshop 5]

1. How would you define the Educational Aim of the project?

R.C: This is really a PSE project. It deals with friendships, relationships and also bullying which is a key interest in schools. It also emphasizes the importance of play to young children which can be lost in a lot of schools, and also the importance of the imagination.

2. How was the project devised or developed?

R.C: Geinor came up with the idea of using fairy-tale stories and looking at the Wolf as a key character. She developed ideas for a scenario and these ideas were discussed with Mark Ryan, the writer. He provided a script which was then worked on in rehearsals by Geinor and the actors.

3. How many performances of the project are planned?

R.C: It's about 80.

4. Do you ever re-tour projects? Under what circumstances?

R.C: Yes, we do. Usually this is in response to teacher demand which we find out about through talking to teachers, from the questionnaires they fill out and from our 'Professional Reference Group'. This happens now more than it did years ago. Re-touring is not a financial issue, nor an artistic one. When we re-tour, we are responding to Curriculum needs of the schools rather than artistic needs of the company.

5. To what extent were teachers involved in the choice of material or the development of ideas?

R.C: We have a Professional Reference Group with a membership of fourteen, made up of teachers and Primary Advisors. These are always well attended. At the meetings we take feedback on the work and discuss it and also bring forward plans and ideas for the future. The Group evaluates the work and we work closely with them in developing teachers' resources. After every performance we give out a pack and an evaluation sheet and the responses to these are looked at carefully and responded to – if, for example, the language or the concepts had not been pitched correctly.

6. Does the company attempt to identify the needs of the children when developing projects?

R.C: Yes… Yes. The theme of 'playing' and the importance of play in this project, for example. The needs of the children are always there.

7. How would you describe your relationship with schools and what developments would you like to see?

R.C: I think the relationship with schools is really good, especially in the Swansea area, where the history of the company goes back twenty years. They like our work and they know the company well. They seem to be committed to using our work because we have good communication with them and we do what they require. We make the work relevant to them. At the beginning of each tour we have an INSET process so they can see the work and final adjustments can be made. These are always well attended. As far as developments are concerned, I would like to see Bridgend respond to our work more. Bridgend has only been visited by the company in the past few years, and the relationships are not as fully developed. They weren't part of the remit of the former Theatr West Glamorgan. They tend to be the last to book projects, whereas Swansea and Neath snap them up. We are going to base a future project on a Bridgend story to try and crack this.

8. Do you employ a 'schools liaison' officer and what are the duties of this post?

R.C: Yes, that is my role. My key duties are maintaining contact with the schools. I spend a lot of time working with teachers on the resource packs. I also do the scheduling and booking, organize the INSET days, analyse the questionnaires, coordinate the Professional Reference Group, give talks... I am also involved in one-off workshops with the actors.

9. Do you provide teaching materials/teaching packs and how are these compiled?

R.C: These are done for every show and, as I have mentioned, I coordinate and edit them, but I work closely with teachers in deciding what should be included.

10. Does the project have identified links to Learning Objectives of the National Curriculum?

R.C: We always closely link the work to the Curriculum. It is clearly indicated where there are links to Learning Objectives, Tasks, Key Skills and what resources are needed. We think this is very important for the teachers. For them everything needs to be justified in terms of the Curriculum. But this isn't limiting for us artistically. We feel there is plenty of scope to be creative whilst giving the schools what they need in terms of the Curriculum.

11. Did the project include workshop or participatory elements? YES/NO

If yes, what governed the choice of methodologies?

R.C: We have a short discussion at the end to bring out the main themes, but for this project we haven't thought it necessary to have a workshop. We do sometimes, for example, in a Set Text project for Key Stage 4, we did use a workshop. For infants it is usually a show with some discussion.

If no, why was the decision made not to use participatory elements?

12. Do you have a policy about the use of workshop and/or participatory work?

R.C: There are no rules really; it depends on the needs of the show. We always do half-day performances and, as with this show, there is often audience involvement.

13. What theatrical influences currently affect your performance work?

G.J: I think there is a variety of theatre that influences me. I think images that stick in my head tend to stay with me and influence me, such as an American production of *The Laramie Project* which was three hours of gripping storytelling. I also think the energy and bravado of the National's *Guys and Dolls* was inspirational, and then the inventiveness of *A Street of Crocodiles* by *Theatre de Complicité* was amazing and made me think of the different ways of telling a story. But overall it has to be theatre that has a strong humanist quality to the storytelling.

14. What drama influences currently affect your participatory work?

R.C: I would say there is not one drama influence. I listen to what children and teachers are saying about the work that inspires them in the classroom and devise my own way to create participatory work.

15. What do you feel are the key differences between Theatre for Children and Theatre in Education? *Curriculum*

R.C: For me the key difference is the level of educational support in TIE. Also the additional resources that are offered and the way in which the work fits into the Curriculum.

G.J: I agree. From a production point of view, I am mindful of the Curriculum but it never restrains me creatively because as the teachers tell me year in, year out, they book us for the live theatre experience as well as the educational needs of the schools.

16. Are your current actors specifically trained/experienced in TIE?

R.C: Of the current team, two have had experience of working in TIE and for one it is her first professional job. The company auditions for each project, though some actors might work in more than one project.

17. Is training or experience in drama/TIE an employment criterion when making acting appointments?

R.C: I don't think so, though it would be part of the skills that are being looked at when the decision is made.

18. Are any of your actors teacher trained? Would this be an advantage?

R.C: I am teacher trained, but not the actors. I suppose it would be an advantage, especially in the workshop elements. It is not really necessary for the production itself. Perhaps some courses in education might be useful for the actors. I try to use my experience to help them adapt to the needs of what they will meet in schools.

19. In what ways has TIE practice in your company changed or developed in recent years?

G.J: It has developed in that we are able to target more schools and children than in the past. But I started work as a stage manager for Theatre West Glamorgan, and worked with Tim Baker and Carys Tudor for five years, before becoming a director for the company. Their ethos of providing theatre which is educational and entertaining for all children has influenced me and I would hope that it would continue to be central to the company's work.

20. How confident are you about the future of TIE in Wales?

R.C: Very confident. It has a definite place. It would be a real tragedy if it were lost. Many of the children here today [*at the performance*] were special needs children and the head teacher was saying that they have learnt more today in this hour than they might do in a month of ordinary teaching. There have been times when children who would not even speak have come out of themselves. That really makes it worthwhile. I think if there were to be a threat to the company that there would be an uproar. Teachers would really complain.

21. How confident are you about the future of your company?

R.C: I think we are fairly secure. We have been going now for twenty years and the need is growing. The Curriculum is developing in all sorts of ways and we are careful to respond to these changes. TIE is increasingly needed.

22. In percentage terms what are your sources of funding?

G.J: –

ACW   82.5%

LEA'S 11.5% (Swansea, Neath, Port Talbot & Bridgend)

INCOME FROM SCHOOLS 6%

23. Do you work in both primary and secondary schools? What is the percentage split between the two sectors?

R.C: We work in both sectors, and we work more in the primary sector.

24. How many TIE projects does the company undertake each year?

R.C: There is usually one project for Key Stage One, one for Key Stage Two and one for Key Stage Four each year.

25. Is your company also involved in community or other forms of theatre?

Not currently, though we are planning a project based on *Melangell* next year – a fourth project – and, I think, that may involve some community performances.

26. Is your company involved in INSET training for teachers?

Not beyond the INSET preparation for our own TIE programmes mentioned above.

27. Do you have any further reflections on the current state of TIE in Wales?

G.J: No. I think I am in a very privileged position to create plays for children, to present productions for young people and to provide the opportunity for them to see live theatrical performances that they may not otherwise be able to due to financial or geographic restraints. I think the enhancement in funding has been well over due, but I do believe it is not merely a case of giving us a big cheque. It's nice to have it, but I believe the mindset within the arts industry has to change and for us not to be seen as the poor country cousin, but as the driving force behind and the future for new audiences and professionals of theatre in Wales.

Name of Company: *Spectacle Theatre* **Title of project:** *Where's Andy?*
Date of Visit: 28/06/04 **Interviewee:** Steve Davies **Position:** Director [via e-mail]
Duration of Project: 45 minutes [Performance 30   Workshop 15]

1. How would you define the Educational Aim of the project?

The educational aims of the project were to provide young children (3-7) with a theatre experience that explored the relationship between safety and freedom. This is a major concern of the audience wanting to explore the wider world and to take risks, and yet not knowing the real dangers that exist. For instance not wanting to hold a parent's hand whilst walking alongside a busy road. We also wanted to develop the skills of literacy: reading and writing and oracy (listening and speaking) through empowerment of young children. This was achieved by giving every child who attended the performance a sticker and cartoon comic that retold the story. It was anticipated that when the child went home a parent or guardian would remark on the badge and the book and a conversation would follow. The child had the advantage in having experienced the live theatre event and could draw upon this experience in the conversation. We wanted to introduce young children to theatre and particularly the fun of theatre. We developed a highly visual style for the production which wittily used a great deal of re-cycled items and materials.

2. How was the project devised or developed?

A brief was given to the writer by the director to write a story that explored safety and freedom for young children. This story was then written as a play and had the title *The Lazy Ant*. This production toured successfully in Wales and was adapted for performance in Lithuania. Wishing to maintain the character of Angharad the Ant, we asked the writer to write another play: 'the further adventures of Angharad the Ant'. We also were aware we needed a new marketing ploy to get back into the schools that enjoyed the original play. Whilst teachers thoroughly enjoyed the Lazy Ant perhaps they would be more interested in having another story. The pupils were obviously older.

3. How many performances of the project are planned?

The company is currently able to continue touring the play to meet demand. It started touring in July 2004 and is being performed in Repertory with *The Clock*. Both plays are scheduled to finish touring at the international young people's theatre festival *Agor Drysau*. If there is sufficient demand the project will be reworked and continue touring. Number of performances currently stands at ninety five.

4. Do you ever re-tour projects? Under what circumstances?

The additional funding the company has received from the WAG through the Arts council has enabled us to tour productions for longer and revisit previous productions. This is a new concept for the company. We are evaluating this over the next two years.

5. To what extent were teachers involved in the choice of material or the development of ideas?

The director worked with teachers by attending class lessons to see how teachers teach story. Workshops with the audience target age range were held with the actors, children designers, writers etc.

6. Does the company attempt to identify the needs of the children when developing projects?

Yes. This is key to the company's work as well as the belief in the beneficial experience of theatre in allowing us to risk-take in a safe environment. The child's understanding of story and how this differs in areas that suffer from multiple deprivation is also an important aspect in developing the production.

7. How would you describe your relationship with schools and what developments would you like to see?

We have a strong and positive relationship with schools. There are however some schools that, for whatever reason, have never booked a theatre company. We are currently attempting to identify such schools and to develop a policy to ensure children in those schools are able to access their entitlement to live theatre.

8. Do you employ a 'schools liaison' officer and what are the duties of this post?

No. That role is divided up between the Artistic Director, the administrator and the Marketing Officer. The duties include maintaining an up-to-date knowledge of current teaching practice and school practice, changes in education practice and how this affects schools, as well as changes to school timetables.

9. Do you provide teaching materials/teaching packs and how are these compiled?

Yes. With *Where's Andy?* each child received a comic book drawn by a local artist and written by the playwright. *The Clock* has a teachers' resource pack developed by the company for teachers.

10. Does the project have identified links to Learning Objectives of the National Curriculum?

Yes, in terms of the Personal and Social Development curriculum. There is much in the project and the experience of the visit to the school that teachers can draw upon to tie into the curriculum.

11. Did the project include workshop or participatory elements? YES/NO

If yes, what governed the choice of methodologies?

Yes, at the end of the play. The actors talk with the children to enable them to begin to individually and collectively make sense of the experience. The audience is free to express their own thoughts and feelings. These are acknowledged and shared. We always turn the questions back to the audience for them to answer for themselves. It is not for us to make the meaning, but to enquire of them what meaning the experience held for the audience. We also draw out the difference between playing a character and being who we are; the difference between fiction and reality. This can often be a difficult area with this age group and is sometimes best left alone. We also ensure photographs can be taken with the actors and the pupils for a record of the visit.

If no, why was the decision made not to use participatory elements?

12. Do you have a policy about the use of workshop and/or participatory work?

Yes. Each production is explored in a different manner and workshops can last ten minutes or a half-day. The function of the workshop is for the audience to begin to make sense of the experience privately and publicly. We create theatre that can be touched, and we recognise the audience's part in the production. Meaning is made by the audience, and we are interested in the meaning they make from it. We do not tour 'messages' except for our belief in theatre as a universally beneficial experience.

13. What theatrical influences currently affect your performance work?

David Mamet , Kantor and the Theatre of the Dead.

14. What drama influences currently affect your participatory work?

The work of the TIE Company Leeds. This company has a long history of participatory work.

15. What do you feel are the key differences between Theatre for Children and Theatre in Education?

It is very difficult to respond to this question. I can think of "Where's Andy?" as TIE or as Theatre for Children. The question is, is it effective in what it sets out to do? If it is, let's not bother with the handle.

16. Are your current actors specifically trained/experienced in TIE?

No. The assistant director is. The current actors have expressed a strong interest in TIE. I have found it very difficult to recruit any actor with any training in TIE unless they have experience from other companies.

17. Is training or experience in drama/TIE an employment criterion when making acting appointments?

It is always a question. I always want people who have expressed a strong interest in TIE. They also need to like young people and be able to act.

18. Are any of your actors teacher trained? Would this be an advantage?

Sometimes they are. Some of the core company members were teachers. We rely on our current knowledge of theatre from practising teachers and Advisors.

19. In what ways has TIE practice in your company changed or developed in recent years?

An increase in funding has enabled us to strengthen the core team. This has enabled us to re-evaluate the entire company and its practise. The infrastructure has developed from the collective decision making process of company members to the Artistic Director-led company. This has altered the company and its practise. The work is of a much higher standard, artistically, educationally and socially. The company still continues to develop and is very forward looking in its approach to theatre making. It ensures that young practitioners have access to the company and responsibility for driving the work forward. The practice continues to take risks and to be innovative in presentation. The company ensures that its work is actually representative of its audience and can be culturally recognised.

20. How confident are you about the future of TIE in Wales?

Very. Training is however a key issue.

21. How confident are you about the future of your company?

I am confident in the company. We live in a constantly changing arts world where security and continuity can never be taken for granted.

22. In percentage terms what are your sources of funding?

Arts Council of Wales 80%
Earned Income   10%
LEA   10%

23. Do you work in both primary and secondary schools? What is the percentage split between the two sectors?

We ensure coverage across Key Stages One, Two and Three. Each two-year block each Key Stage gets a third share. We also tour to youth centres and the wider community.

24. How many TIE projects does the company undertake each year?

This year four, next year three new projects plus continuation of two from this year.

25. Is your company also involved in community or other forms of theatre?

Yes. Youth Theatre, Community Theatre and Community Arts.

26. Is your company involved in INSET training for teachers?

Yes. We are involved in INSET in all manner of ways. Sometimes it is project-related and at other times it is skill-based training. It does get trickier as the years progress, mainly due to changes within the education system and problems getting teachers released or provided with cover. It can never be planned in these days as a matter of course.

27. Do you have any further reflections on the current state of TIE in Wales?

Without TIE over the last thirty years in Wales, what would the theatre scene in Wales look like today? Its development of actors, writers, directors, designers etc has made an enormous contribution to Welsh Theatre and Culture. It needs to be recognised and the personnel within it need recognition by the wider arts scene for TIE's massive contribution to culture in Wales and internationally.

Name of Company: *Theatr Clwyd TIE* **Title of project:** *The Mabinogion*
Date: 16/06/04 **Interviewee:** Tim Baker **Position:** Director
Duration of Project: Full day [Performance 70 mins Workshop 120 mins]

1. How would you define the Educational Aim of the project?

It's in the realm of imagination and the need to have stories within your community. You suddenly realize that these fantasies are necessary as part of the need for escapism. What are your local stories? What are your myths? What are your legends? And why do we need them? We need to explain certain things that happen around our lives, because when you are in a non-scientific age you need to search for things that the rational side hasn't arrived at yet. An image I worked with with the actors early on was that if you don't know what a rainbow is, then what it is has all sorts of possible connotations. [The project] doesn't have a direct educational aim in a curriculum sense, unlike, say, our project on the Tudors last year which was about the world of the Tudors and what they believed. The Victorian project was very specific – the world of the Victorians and their attitudes towards status, class and so on and so forth. There are debates in there but that isn't the same in the *Mabinogion*. Having said that I think it is important for children to experience something of that world, in particular something of theatrical technique that goes towards making stories. If anything, I have been almost less defined about specific educational aims in this project because I want the kids to have a total experience.

2. How was the project devised or developed?

We read the stories over and over again. We did a lot of research into what storytelling is about. There's a hidden language in these stories, such as that there are always things in threes; first this and then that and finally that. There are lots of patterns like that and other things such as if you see a white beast when you are hunting it is usually a portal into the other world – stuff like that. The core company in addition to the actors was me, the designer, the composer and choreographer. It was that foursome that initially started dissecting the stories and setting down ideas – 'that could be a dance, that could be a lullaby, that could be a…'. Then we essentially devised it by storyboarding it and then improvising it. We really had difficulty with, in improvisatory terms, with language. It's hard. You can improvise everyday vernacular okay, but when it gets to using heightened language, or you've got figures that are slightly mythical so they don't… they don't have 'jabber' – you know what I mean?

Did you end up with a script then?

Yes, yes. Definitely, which I wrote.

3. How many performances of the project are planned?

Ten a week for four weeks. Forty performances.

4. Do you ever re-tour projects? Under what circumstances?

Yes, we do it a lot. I'm pleased to say that a lot of the stuff has been very successful and very popular. In relation to the Key Stage Two material, we've done history projects for the last four years and, of course, they don't age. So it is prudent in artistic and financial terms to bring stuff back. Generally it's a 70 per cent/30 per cent ratio, so that 70 per cent is new and 30 per cent is coming back. What we haven't done is shared that idea by playing in other counties on another patch.

Is that something you'd like to do?

Yes, yes. Very much, very much.

5. To what extent were teachers involved in the choice of material or the development of ideas?

We have a group, a teachers' group where we share ideas. We also have a group which is made up of the Arts Development Officers for the three old counties of Clwyd: Denbigh, Wrexham and Flintshire. They are a sort of monitoring/advisory group and it's through them that we would say, 'here's the Mabinogion, what do you think?' and they would say, 'yep, we can see that working'. In fact, this year, for the first time they are doing the bookings for us. They are selecting schools that they think would benefit. Because with the new funding, the cost to schools is going down and the take-up is going up. Therefore the decision about who gets the show… it needs to be less about who's quickest off the mark on Monday morning and more about who needs it.

6. Does the company attempt to identify the needs of the children when developing projects?

That's a very good question, because our clients in the end are the children, although the teachers make the decisions. I do what we call a 'Trojan Horse' thing, whereby the marketing package for the play (the *Mabinogion* isn't a very good example) is to the teachers. For example, *Flora's War* was ostensibly about home life during World War Two, but actually it was about truth and lies in families. The selling point for the teachers is World War Two, but I don't really care if the kids know much about World War Two. What I do care about is what happens to families under stress. *Flora's War* was all about the need for truth in relationships against the news' lies and that truth is the first casualty of war. At the beginning of every project, including this one, we go and spend time in every school with the kids to try and get a little bit into their world.

7. How would you describe your relationship with schools and what developments would you like to see?

I would really like to see the schools, and this applies to the building as much as the department, really seeing us as a resource. It's something to do with communication. For example, all my rehearsals are open, all my technical rehearsals are open, but we could go a lot further. And because we are less physically performing in schools than other companies (although we are in schools 50 per cent of the year) it would be good to think that we could do school-specific projects such as a residency in a school. I think the balance to be struck is to respond to schools' needs so they can dictate what they are getting.

8. Do you employ a 'schools liaison' officer and what are the duties of this post?

Jane [Meakins]'s role is Educational Support Worker. She is essentially schools liaison and the deliverer of workshops. There is a whole workshop programme outside of the project. Jane is in school most days of the year. We also now have an Educational Producer whose job it is to work on long-term plans and so on.

9. Do you provide teaching materials/teaching packs and how are these compiled?

Yes, yes we do. They are usually compiled by me with Jane.

10. Does the project have identified links to Learning Objectives of the National Curriculum?

Not in this project. Usually Learning Objectives within the Key Stages are identified. For this project, knowledge of Welsh culture is part of the Curriculum but the links aren't quite as 'spiky' as they have been in the past – it doesn't slot straight in.

11. Did the project include workshop or participatory elements? YES/NO

If yes, what governed the choice of methodologies?

We do sometimes use the traditional workshop at the end of the play. It's worked out this way because of the number of performances we wanted and the fact that it's a day-long project with an A and B side to it. The workshop in this one is much more drama-orientated but that's got huge value, I think, in terms of the way that teachers might want to take it on and use it. We 'sub-contracted' [the workshop] essentially through Jane [Meakin] so there's me working on the show and Jane working on the workshop.

Did the workshop leader take part in the devising process?

Essentially she was following Jane's template.

If no, why was the decision made not to use participatory elements?

12. Do you have a policy about the use of workshop and/or participatory work?

It just depends on the needs of the project. What I suppose I champion here more than anything else, though there are no hard rules, is performance. I am not of the view that a participatory element is [a] essential to TIE, neither do I believe that [b] the young people in that performance you saw today were not participating. Again, it does come partly from working in a building. The building stands for the values of performance, otherwise why build theatres? While it exists you have to understand that its *raison d'être* right through the whole catchment area and in political circles is about getting people into this space. Even sometimes when you are in a school there's a feeling, 'well, why aren't we in the theatre?' It's a different thing to working in, for example, Neath where there isn't a decent theatre in the area.

13. What theatrical influences currently affect your performance work?

What affects me is the need for very high production values and simplicity of storytelling. That applies to much of the work on the main stage here as well, for example, *To Kill a Mocking Bird* and a lot of the shows I've done here. Big spaces, big plays, but simple construction. In this one we wanted to go into certain areas like puppetry and so on, but actually when Lynn [Hunter] is actually just sitting talking to the kids about the loss of the child, it is just as good for me as all the other stuff. I'll be interested to see what other people say to that question!

14. What drama influences currently affect your participatory work?

This might be a question for Jane. I mean [the drama theorists] are there. I always have admired Dorothy Heathcote in relation to entering the world of a particular piece of work. Boal in relation to Forum Theatre less so. I'll tell you what has really influenced me – a sort of back-door answer to it – I have been very lucky over the last five or six years to direct some major twentieth-century texts – a piece for the National Theatre, two or three years ago I worked on *Oh What a Lovely War* here and the work of Dario Fo. Going to these major figures of the twentieth century who've got massive theories about how theatre works for children – you can't help it rubbing off. You can't do *Lovely War* without looking at Joan Littlewood's life and work. You can't do Brecht without looking at Brecht from the beginning to the end, more or less. And all that rubs off in terms of the way that theatre works, should work. One thing I've learned is that you can't let yourself get bogged down in conventions. Theatre works because it works – when it works.

15. What do you feel are the key differences between Theatre for Children and Theatre in Education?

That is either a 'non-question' or it is *the* question. I've come through a tradition, as you know, a whole exploration of what TIE is and what Theatre for Children is and what the theatre experience for young people is. I think my response to the question is – and this isn't to do with Theatr Clwyd at all – it's to do with an experience or a set of experiences I had maybe six or seven years ago. I began to realize that what we might have been offering to young people in its best and worst form might have been a stunning educational experience but was doing nothing to address the hunger that I want them to have for the medium. To take a musical analogy, it's great to go in and deconstruct an opera and look at it and be around a musician playing an instrument and looking at form and content or whatever – but that would never be a substitute for seeing an opera. And if it's a substitute for that – and that's the only experience they get – then you are robbing kids of one of the elements of the medium that we are here to serve, our love of performance. I would take that even further – a love of performance in a dedicated space. If we are bringing up a generation of young people whose only experience of theatre is (and I mean no disrespect by saying this) is of actors in a school hall with two planks and a box (which I love), but if that's their only experience then what are we doing to them in terms of inspiring a hunger for the medium and then becoming writers, becoming actors, becoming an audience and a hankering for change? It's particularly true being here because

Tim Baker

this audience is relatively middle class and relatively narrow in its taste. I want to create an audience coming up through which is hungry for more stuff. How that defines Children's Theatre and TIE, I don't know. I really can't define TIE in terms of the Curriculum – because that's not true. I can't define Children's Theatre by saying it's got no content because I don't like that either. It's really difficult. We call our department "YPT/TIE" which is a kind of wallpaper really. But the Key Stage Three project we are going to be doing in October is very specifically a piece about peer pressure and career choice. That goes into the school with four actors, kids in a circle, and it hits hard. It's got a big debate element in it. The kids are working with the actors before the show. They go in, see a piece, they come out, they advise the actors, and they go back in. It's got a really traditional feel to it. I suppose that the answer to your question is that the form and the content are very interlinked.

16. Are your current actors specifically trained/experienced in TIE?

No. Well, some of them are – like Lynn.

17. Is training or experience in drama/TIE an employment criterion when making acting appointments?

No… no it's not. What is important, though, which I think is part of the training, is that they are hungry for being more than just actors; that they are hungry to be facilitators and also devisors. The key thing about this show is that it is a devised piece. I deliberately take actors through that process. The actor goes into the process, particularly young actors just out of drama school, as an actor-centred actor and hopefully they come out as a show-centred actor because it is part of the whole process.

18. Are any of your actors teacher trained? Would this be an advantage?

That's a really good question. [_musing_] Teacher trained? I certainly wouldn't want to substitute teacher training for actor training. I really wouldn't, because I think that there's something about actor's training which is important, although I think the advantage of both is huge. But I think that thing that we used to call 'actor/teacher' is a changed thing by now. It's not a term I would use now. It's because, it's a shame, but a lot of these terminologies within the profession have got tarnished. When I do work at the Welsh College I pick up this 'TIE thing' [_giving a look of disdain_] from young actors who haven't even left college, you know. I'm really pushing this thing of how important theatre for young people is. And I shun the 'actor/teacher' term partly because it's been over-laundered, I think.

19. In what ways has TIE practice in your company changed or developed in recent years?

In the last five years, if anything, it's got a little less Curriculum-based. Five years ago, all companies were fighting very, very hard for their survival, and what happens when you are fighting for survival is that your work has to be seen to be more needed. This was happening a lot, and you start to do stuff which is smack in the centre of the Curriculum because you are charging higher prices for the work and so on. I talk a lot to Kevin [Lewis] from Theatr Iolo and he tends to say 'book this for kids – it's exciting' and the content thing gets in the way of that sometimes because of the Curriculum demand for overt educational content.

20. How confident are you about the future of TIE in Wales?

In one way I am very confident because, at last, we can breathe – a little bit – in terms of the funding. I am not confident that the Arts Council has taken the theory right the way through because in the new funding round they haven't corrected the old underfunding. They've given everybody a fair slice of the cake, but you've still got, for example, Na N'og (my old company of West Glamorgan) whose baseline is £165,000, whereas the baseline here is £86,000. We're nearly £100,000 out in relation to them. Frân Wen is poor in relation to Spectacle as well. The north is poor in the baseline funding – not the new money–in comparison to the south. I think that there is a healthier atmosphere. We've been real enemies in some years – I mean shouting across the table – and the franchise bid did nothing to help that. We don't have a shared methodology and practice. It's very disparate. I think that there is potential for this new agency. It could make it work. Hopefully what still is there – even if the gaps are there – is in the practice. You know, I, sadly, haven't seen, for example, a Theatr Powys' piece, and they haven't seen a piece of my work, for a long time. That's appalling. And I could cite two pieces of work that I've seen in the last year and a half from different companies – Welsh companies – that I won't name – that I wouldn't have anywhere near here. I wouldn't have in any of the schools here. Really poor pieces of work. Poor pieces of content. Poor debates and poor performance standards. And if they score negatively on all those counts for me... One thing I should have said earlier is that over the years I've become more and more conscious of the damage that poor TIE can do. It's one thing to say, 'you should be in schools, you should be whatever, whatever, whatever' but above all, I really do think, if a bad experience is had by the kids – whether in terms of quality, content, leadership, whatever, and it's called 'theatre' ('that's theatre Johnny'), the damage that that does is irreparable. And I have seen some bad work. So when you get to this whole thing of exchanging work, we've got to keep improving our work. And the really dismal thing about it is that we're not getting together enough, and I blame myself for that. Partly because we're always busy, but also because it's still very rare that there's new people coming through. I mean the bulk of theatre in education in Wales, 90 per cent maybe, of it is being directed by Gary Meredith, Steve Davies, Gaynor Jones, Ian Yeoman, so on and so forth. No disrespect to any of us, but where's the next body of people hungry for our jobs?

21. How confident are you about the future of your company?

There's one battle that I've won here – that I'm slowly winning, slowly. When I came here five years ago, there was this monster called 'Theatr Clwyd's great productions in the main theatre and Emlyn Williams'! And there was a little tributary here called 'the TIE'. And no one went to see these shows. They didn't really care about the shows, and the costumes were usually made by the stage manager. And now, it's *in there* [*the theatre*]. And it's properly resourced so that the entire resources of the wardrobe, the LX, the costumes and so on, go towards the production in the same way and at the same standards as they would do anywhere else. So what I hope I've done here, is to try to change perception of the road that leads to building an audience. Before I got here, the real audience started at twenty, twenty-one. Now it starts at eight or whatever. And that's a big thing. So, I think, while I've been here that's been built into the ethos of the building now. I don't think it will go. So while Theatr Clwyd rolls on, it's not the Russian Doll anymore – we're fully part of it. Having said that, as you probably know, Theatr Clwyd is volatile because of its heavy reliance on Flintshire after the old Clwyd disappeared and, also, it's got aspirations to move and have a Cardiff base, become a National Theatre. What happens to the young people's operation here should that happen? I don't know. Bear in mind that the production team is not just in TIE – it's serving ALL the productions. Anything that goes out from here has an education package with it. All our touring work has an education package. When a tour goes out it will have a dedicated education support worker on tour with the company with a workshop everyday. We run summer schools here, we run weekly workshops. The actual operation of the department is very big. So the educational work in terms of its servicing role with the main theatre will, I think, go on. It's been a feature of arts funding here, so I'm fairly confident.

22. In percentage terms what are your sources of funding?

The current budget consists of something like 56 per cent ACW grant. Twenty-one per cent comes from Flintshire. The rest of it is box office and sponsorship of about 11 per cent or 12 per cent. The sponsorship is mainly from banks and is not separated out in budgeting terms. The heating, lighting and so on just comes out of the central budget of Theatr Clwyd. The sticking point has been that ever since Clwyd was split up, Denbighshire and Wrexham have said, 'no, we're not paying, because… you're not on our patch'. It's really hard in terms of new money. Flintshire want some kind of extra benefit because 'we are putting money in', but the Arts Council new money has to be spent equally throughout old Clwyd.

23. Do you work in both primary and secondary schools? What is the percentage split between the two sectors?

It's about equal. We used to do storytelling in schools for Key Stage One. This project is for Key Stage Two. The project I mentioned earlier will be for Key Stage Three and there will be a performance piece for Key Stage Four. This year we've done a production for Key Stage One. Of the four Key Stages two are in schools and two are here.

24. How many TIE projects does the company undertake each year?

Four. Four a year and possibly a 'bring back' which is dependent upon sponsorship. Barclays have expressed an interest in the *Mabinogion,* so we might bring it back next spring, but that hangs on the money from Barclays.

25. Is your company also involved in community or other forms of theatre?

I am, but the actors are on short-term contracts. The aim next year is to have a company. We hope to have a nine-month contract and that then starts to answer some of your other questions. They will have a community brief and a training brief. The trouble is you can't train actors up in a four-week rehearsal period. The main thing we want to aim for is personnel continuity. All the stuff that I feel we are really about is about being in a company, to take stuff to conferences, to have a company ethos, a company voice, a company discipline or whatever. When you are just casting up for one show, it doesn't have the same ethos.

26. Is your company involved in INSET training for teachers?

Yes. Yes. We do days of 'how you can use our work' or 'what theatre means'. We're trying to do more. We are also quite heavily involved in arts and business training.

27. Do you have any further reflections on the current state of TIE in Wales?

No, I don't think so, Rog. Thank you.

Name of Company: *Theatr Powys*   **Title of project:** *Pow Wow*
Date of Visit: 20/08/04 **Interviewee:** Ian Yeoman **Position:** Artistic Director
Duration of Project: Full Day [Performance/Workshop 180 mins approx.]

1. How would you define the Educational Aim of the project?

The programme is called *Pow Wow – the Power of the Circle.* We're working with years one and two, so the educational aim was to develop social responsibility, communication, implication and to ritualize that. Also to place this in a context of our relationship with nature and each other and particularly our relationship to the young because they are becoming responsible for the future. Educationally it does say something about native North Americans and indigenous populations and things like that, but just as important was how we 'can be together' and 'be with the planet'.

2. How was the project devised or developed?

We never looked at the old script! The initial thought in choosing the programme was the original *Pow Wow* programme had a tepee inside a fence, and a cowboy who was a showman, like a Bill Hickok. I thought that had quite a strong resonance to Guantanamo Bay and an ongoing relationship between people, showmen, and indigenous populations all over the world now. So that was what attracted myself and the company to it. We did a lot of research into particularly the Sioux Indians and the massacre of 'Wounded Knee'. Since then of course Wounded Knee became a reservation, well it exists within a reservation. And there was a place called the Carlisle Industrial School for Native American children. There was a particular guy who set up a school and, essentially, they took the young people off the reservations and stuck them in school and they westernized everything, Christianized their names, cut off their hair, changed their clothing, made them wear shoes and there's a very involved, pretty tragic story involved in all of that. So the two concepts were how originally they would relate to their history and to their 'natural condition' and, then, having gone out into the world, they were sent to school. We wanted to see how the very young people that we're dealing with would attempt to, if you like, square the circle. To come to understand what was going on in that situation.

The working process consisted of a lot of depictive work. I don't tend to ever set improvisations. I always try and set depictive, still, concrete moments, because I think then people can distil what they're understanding about a question. Then, if you have enough depictive moments you start to discover how you can start to bleed them all together. I've never been a great fan of open improvisation.

3. How many performances of the project are planned?

We had two companies on the road for six weeks, generally five a week. That's sixty performances, and then this coming term it tours for another six weeks. Eighteen weeks in total. Ninety performances.

4. Do you ever re-tour projects? Under what circumstances?

Since I've been at Theatr Powys, we haven't re-toured a junior school programme; they've all been new. On two occasions we have re-toured secondary school work. We re-toured *The Apothecary's Story* [which was rooted in the

Romeo and Juliet material] and we re-toured *Something that Happened Just South of Solitude*. The reason for that was, I think, that we felt really happy with the work and we knew there would be a demand, which there was. And I think it deserved a bit more exposure, because you can work quite hard to produce something and then, you know, in the space of five or six weeks, it can disappear.

With the junior schools we always know that we will book out. With secondary schools there is a much more particular difficulty in getting into the schools and getting young people off their Curriculum for a full day – and in bigger schools even for two days. So the work has to be 'relevant'. We're in that contradiction about 'how does this relate to their Curriculum and their examinations' etc. So it's a very fine balance between producing something that the schools think will apply to what they are having to deliver and producing something that goes beyond, you know, 'handy hints for examinations'!

5. To what extent were teachers involved in the choice of material or the development of ideas?

Very little. I would say that's a policy. If we were simply to ask the teachers to suggest material – and then be obliged to respond – I think it would reduce the impact of the company's work. That's not a sexy position to hold, but I think it's true.

6. Does the company attempt to identify the needs of the children when developing projects?

All the time. All the time. For example, the company was invited into a school to do an eleven-week ongoing project, last year, because in years three and four anti-social behaviour in the school was extreme. The school applied for money to use drama as a way of coping with the behaviour that was evident. So, *Pow Wow – the Power of the Circle*, as a general tool is clearly an attempt to humanize the way in which young people communicate with each other. And that's a real need. The Steinbeck work, the *Solitude* programme, was an attempt to make that story meaningful. And we all know, I think, that they get whipped through book after book and text after text, and the relevance or resonance is seldom attended to. So we try to deal with whatever we think is being posed for them, if that makes sense.

7. How would you describe your relationship with schools and what developments would you like to see?

I think that the company's relationship with the junior schools is an excellent one. Relating back to your question about whether we refer to teachers, we don't, very often, but we always have more demand than we can meet, so I think that the junior schools are extremely happy with what we produce and they get an enormous amount out of it. Secondary schools are slightly more difficult. We recently held a meeting with the Head Teachers Association and we pointed out that there was one school that hadn't booked in 33 years, I think, since the birth of Theatr Powys. And there are one or two schools that book us every now and again. And the balance between what's on offer and the pressure on the schools is something that I still think needs working on. It's easier not to book because you don't disrupt the schedule. I think we have an extremely good relationship with the secondary schools with whom we consistently work. But I think there's still work to do. And that poses questions for the company – about the nature of the work. If you make the work more attractive, or more applicable to what their pressure is, then you might be advised to do half-day programmes, or just hour-long programmes and then it would be much easier. What we are trying to do is convince the schools to have us for a full day.

8. Do you employ a 'schools liaison' officer and what are the duties of this post?

No. It did at one point, I believe, before I became part of the company. But we have an administrative and general manager facility that is extremely knowledgeable. They are not only *au fait* with what the company does, but *au fait* with how schools operate. So all of the current relationship – bookings, discussions, presentation of what we do – is conducted through the general manger and the artistic director. The value of having a 'liaison officer' would be to have a person who is a practitioner and who would be going into schools doing more work, follow-up and workshops in developmental terms. But, objectively, we don't have the money to do that.

9. Do you provide teaching materials/teaching packs and how are these compiled?

We do, on occasions. And we haven't on occasions. And the most honest answer to that would be that they are produced by myself in collaboration with the actors. But when you are devising and rehearsing and getting out in four or five weeks and all the work is original, sometimes that can slip. We've produced, I think, some really exciting junior school packs, and we have produced one or two very exciting secondary school packs, but on occasions we end up with no support materials. How can we tolerate that, or how can I tolerate that? The answer relates to the fact that I know, particularly in the secondary school sector, that we could expend vast energy producing a teacher's resource materials that will never be employed because, almost as soon as you've gone, they're back into what they need to do. They might be extremely interested but... it's impossible. In junior schools I think we could develop this more. We recently did a most interesting programme – I think you saw it – *To a Mouse* – all we produced was a storybook and many, many, many teachers have phoned us up saying 'my storybook is battered, have you got another copy?' Now that's an important resource.

10. Does the project have identified links to Learning Objectives of the National Curriculum?

My absolute knowledge of the National Curriculum for Key Stage One is probably not very up to date. Insofar as Key Stage One is about oral expression, communication, self-discipline, sociability, other cultures – insofar as it is then I think the answer's 'yes'. But at no point did we sit down and diagnose what the needs of Key Stage One are. We never did that.

11. Did the project include workshop or participatory elements? YES/NO

If yes, what governed the choice of methodologies?

Putting young people, particularly very young people, in an entirely verbal mode of communication doesn't sit satisfactorily in relation to their stage of development. Young children's classrooms are full of practical, 'manipulable' things – sandpits, plasticine. So we wanted to allow them to express themselves as instinctively and artistically as they could. Through play. But then, in the performance, to see their creations, the product of what they have done together, being recognized and developed and brought through in the story. We put, and I always put, a lot of emphasis on music, because that is another very instinctive way of communicating ideas, I think. And at other times it did become discursive and verbal but by then, hopefully, the investment in the thing gives them a reason to want to say things. In a nutshell I think the overall methodology we try and apply is 'if you are going to ask young people to try and do something they have to have an investment in the doing of it'. Too many times they're asked to write things or say things or answer things and actually they don't have the investment. That's a complete disassociation from what we do in real life. You only write the letter if you need to write the letter. You get hold of something if you want and need to get hold of it. We try and present contexts where we create the motivation to do the thing.

If no, why was the decision made not to use participatory elements?

12. Do you have a policy about the use of workshop and/or participatory work?

Yes. I'm very proud to say – and that's not an individual pride – that I do believe that we are one of the very few companies in the United Kingdom that still adhere to those kinds of educational methodologies. Now that's not just a pat on the back for the individuals who have made up the company throughout its history. It has also been the product of the ongoing support of the County Council and the Arts Council in partnership. Too many companies were squeezed, and then too many individuals caved in and, therefore, there's a great deal less participatory drama methodology at work. Your previous work, *Paradigm Lost* (which I think is a great title), speaks about that. So, yes, it's a policy. It's a policy that is rooted in the history of the company. To be absolutely honest, I think there was a phase in the early to mid-90s where, yes, it was still being adhered to, but it was slipping away. There was much higher emphasis being placed on high-level production value performance work. I think, and again this isn't completely individual, that since I've been here, we have learned more and placed more emphasis on drama methodology.

13. What theatrical influences currently affect your performance work?

I think that in a lot of the theatre work that I do, even within TIE (and we also do community theatre), I have always had a fear of social realist, naturalistic, 'these are kids having a tough time', 'what are the issues involved?' kind of stuff. I think my work, Theatr Powys' work, is influenced quite a lot by European kinds of approaches. I'm interested in movement and I'm interested in music and I'm interested in stillness and I'm interested in depictions. I'm not interested in trying to put *Coronation Street* on stage which is what I honestly believe that some approaches to young people's work are trying to do.

14. What drama influences currently affect your participatory work?

I can always identify the influences because without the influences it probably wouldn't exist. But it's not a litany. And it's not a simple case of applying someone else's thinking. The Bolton/Heathcote drama heritage is very important, but that has been developed and shifted through many other practitioners. Tony Grady who died recently, Margaret Higgins who is a drama teacher, Maggie Hulson who is a drama teacher and the ongoing work of NATD all influence the company. Educationally and theatrically speaking, then, people like Geoff Gillham, of course. But then there's musicians. I'm not being very concise now, but sometimes influences can feel very 'dead', whereas actually the people I am working with are having an immediate affect upon me. Daniel Lawrence, who's a musician-composer, people I'm working with now, all the members of the company. Emyr Bell, who's a Welsh TIE practitioner, spent seven years with the company. And over seven years he learnt an enormous amount, but over seven years he started to influence what I did. Those influences are not dead; they're not dead things. If we are talking theoretically, I still think the highest level of theoretical influence is to do with people like Tag MacEntegart, David Davis. I still think that it's the people who have been interested in the relation of theatre and drama to learning, or the people who are interested in learning which you can then apply to theatre and drama, which

Ian Yeoman, Theatr Powys.

provide the profoundest influence. But, then, I am a product of so many of these different influences and in a sense I become an influence on the people that I work with. I wouldn't claim to be a theoretician in the same way, but I am a practitioner that can employ those influences in a particular way within TIE.

15. What do you feel are the key differences between Theatre for Children and Theatre in Education?

I have absolutely no time for the argument that there is a blurring between the two. The key differences are clear and have been clear since theatre in education was invented. The fact that people want to obfuscate the key differences is another question, but I don't think that there's a practical historical blurring. Theatre for Children is where you perform a play for children, or young people, and is an absolutely valid and creditable thing. But in theatre in education you are applying the kinds of methodologies that we've been discussing – consciously alongside the theatre, to involve them interactively and spiritually, but also to allow them the practice that affects the product of the process. There's no blurring in that; it's either that you continue to try to develop that as a practice or you don't. I don't believe that you can do it particularly effectively with a large audience. With primary schools we work with maximum numbers of forty. In secondary schools we work with maximum numbers of two classes which can be anything up to sixty or seventy people. Even that is extremely difficult, unless you really know what you are trying to do. But you can promote ideas, you can set up situations, but then they have to have a purchase, they have to have a practice, they have to be enabled to make a contribution. Or, they are simply an audience who watch the play and are, or are not, provoked by what is in the play. The concept of doing an hour-long play and then having a hot seat is sometimes called 'theatre in education'. Actually, 90 per cent of the questions in the hot seat are about 'who made you costumes?' or 'how did you learn your lines?' or 'how did you do that bit?' Unless you create conditions where kids can discuss the content, then they won't. They might go away thinking about it but there's no social interaction. Theatre in Education is about young people being responsible for their own, and others, relationship to the material.

16. Are your current actors specifically trained/experienced in TIE?

To relative degrees. We had two companies on the road. One of the actor/teachers is exceptionally experienced. But, coincidentally, the company has recently employed two core actor/teachers who have very little experience.

17. Is training or experience in drama/TIE an employment criterion when making acting appointments?

You know when you have 'essential' and 'desirable' categories? [when inviting applications] Well, if we applied it as an 'essential' criterion that would be idealism, because training institutions are not training people to do it any more. 'Desirable' would be a knowledge of education, drama in education and the skills that go along with theatre. In an ideal world this would be wonderful. Therefore, what we have become is a company that has a history and a policy, and we have a level of experience already within the company. With new company members we have to engage in the building and re-forging and re-building of practice to protect that theoretical and practical approach to the work.

18. Are any of your actors teacher trained? Would this be an advantage?

Right now? It still happens. In the last three or four years we have worked with quite a number – David Lynn, Meirion Hughes, several. There are numbers of people who are teachers. Danie [Croft], for example, is a very experienced actor/teacher, but has never taught in a classroom. I have never been a classroom teacher. Of course it's an advantage – that's what I mean when I talk about the relationship between educational theory and the drama. But being a classroom teacher does not mean that you will be a good theatre in educationalist. Classroom teachers are now coming out of their training and, to be blunt, a lot of them have been taught the kind of educational theory that applies to the late 1980s and '90s. A lot of classroom teachers don't know very much about the kind of educational approach we take. So being a classroom teacher does not qualify you and being an actor does not qualify you. That kind of hybrid is a rare thing. Personally, I always look for people with a sense of drama and theatre that are interested in young people, rather than look for teachers that are interested in drama or theatre; that's where I put my emphasis.

19. In what ways has TIE practice in your company changed or developed in recent years?

Well, I hope it's getting better. I believe it has become more… utterly committed. I believe that. I believe within the current company we have made real developments in terms of the relationship of the design element of the work to the work as a whole. We no longer have TIE programmes that are just placed on the separate work of the designers. I think we have a much more integrated relationship between the work and setting, props, costume, music and the content of the piece. I am really very happy with that at the moment, though I am not complacent about it.

20. How confident are you about the future of TIE in Wales?

You can't judge it… you can't judge these things because these are political economic questions which are constantly shifting. I am extremely confident about the commitment to support and develop theatre which is designed for young people in Wales. I am extremely confident about that. I have to say I am not at all confident about an ongoing historical development of theatre in education. Now that, once again, brings us to the hoary old definition question. I don't know whether it is useful for me to say any more about that, but the real positives are that there is a real drive to protect work for young people in Wales. That is an enormously positive thing. Whether there is an ongoing interest or enthusiasm or commitment to develop theatre in education as I understand it, I am not at all as confident about. I ask questions like 'why don't we have an MA in Educational Drama and Theatre in Education?' Why, when students go into the drama colleges are they not given proper training in TIE? They might have an option to do a one-off taster session in what is called TIE, but I don't think there is an infrastructure that recognizes the power of that art form and, therefore, young people are not being inculcated with it. Therefore, the research, training and development in TIE are actually happening on the ground. And that's a difficult burden, particularly when you think that sooner or later we will have popped our clogs. And I honestly believe that there is a danger that an entire methodology will go down the Swanee. I believe that… that that is a really imminent possibility.

21. How confident are you about the future of your company?

I am really confident that we can justify everything that we do. I believe that if the redevelopment of the Drama Centre goes ahead that will be a real statement of support from the Arts Council and the Powys County Council. That's a strong position to be in. I am very confident about the company as a whole. I have to say, two weeks ago, a local county councillor, described the company as a white elephant; money wasters who run around the country playing to ten people and expect the taxpayer to pick up the bill. Now, not only is he misinformed, but I believe that he is telling lies. I believe that there is a political agenda at work there. I am always only as confident as conditions lead me to believe. I have no problem with my own confidence in the company and its ability to meet its remit, but developments are always occurring, and a fine level of support and recognition of the company's work can very quickly turn into a very problematic situation, and we must always be prepared for that to occur. But I am pleased and grateful for the ongoing support that we have. I do believe that there are people in positions of authority who genuinely support what we are doing.

22. In percentage terms what are your sources of funding?

It used to be slightly more from the Local Authority, but it has recently shifted and we now get slightly more from the Arts Council, because there has been an increased level of funding for this sector from them. But in principled terms, and that is why we are still offering a free service, I think, as a company in Wales, we are still on a roughly mutual fifty-fifty level of funding. The current companies gratitude or recognition of that goes back to previous people who were extremely clever. There is also some box office, but no sponsorship of the company.

23. Do you work in both primary and secondary schools? What is the percentage split between the two sectors?

We spend more time in junior. This year, eighteen weeks of touring in the junior school sector, and six weeks of touring in the secondary schools.

24. How many TIE projects does the company undertake each year?

Three – a secondary school programme, a junior school programme and a Welsh language programme, which, for the last five or six years, has never been simply translated work. We are about to develop a brand new Welsh-language programme. There is a difference in staffing and approach and application of what we are doing in the Welsh language. It would be easy in this particular area of Wales to develop our TIE work in English and simply translate it. We don't do that. The sources of the methodology are the same, but very few of these, I would argue, have been rooted in Wales. I don't mind being quite honest about that. There is an ongoing living practical influence, but the theoretical influences, I think, have been developed in the post-war era throughout the UK. Within Powys, of course, a large percentage of our Welsh-language constituency for the work is second language units, so even when you are working with fluent, born and bred first-language Welsh actors, they consistently run up against the problem that the capability of the young people to sustain the work that they want is insufficient. We, therefore, have an extremely particular problem educationally about designing work which is interesting and in Welsh, but that doesn't completely leave behind an audience which is struggling with a developing vocabulary. That is something that we talk about a great deal. This might be something about which some people might question my role in that I have very little, zero, Welsh vocabulary. But what I have is a methodology, and I also have an understanding of how you work when you have very little vocabulary. Now that is something as a company we find very fruitful. I would add, I believe, that the relationships that are formed in the company with Welsh practitioners have enabled that to be a valuable, rather than a politically difficult, relationship. But, you'd have to ask them!

25. Is your company also involved in community or other forms of theatre?

Yes. We do one major community tour to community audiences, art centres and theatres, normally around December/January. Seven/eight years ago maybe there was two. We can't afford to do two anymore. And we also have ring-fenced, fought for, dug our heels in and sustained – and not only sustained but developed – the work with young people through the company's youth theatre, which is an ongoing central remit of what we do.

26. Is your company involved in INSET training for teachers?

Yes. Not in a structured way within the county or within the Education Authority. But on numbers of occasions we have responded to such requests. I will run in-service days in the use of drama in the classroom. That is something that I would like to develop further because it can only assist the relations with the schools for what the company does. But, that's an objective thing. Again, there are very few schools who would chose to spend their in-service day introducing drama – they are much more interested in the day-to-day nitty-gritty of what is occurring in the school.

27. Do you have any further reflections on the current state of TIE in Wales?

I think that this sector of work is hugely indebted to the Arts Council, particularly to Francis Medley. I do have a lot of confidence in them. I think that the common strategy to employ a kind of advocate/coordinator is a positive thing, though they failed to make an appointment. That places us with an interesting question – 'who is this person who can do this job?' My own view is that to get the full value of such a post, you are looking for someone with an enormous level of skills and understanding. The fact that that is an ongoing debate is evidence of how confident we can feel about this sector of work, and the importance that is being placed on young people's work. And I think that we are in a process, as companies, of learning to work with each other rather than exist in a kind of star-shaped kind of 'stand-off', where you are all the time looking to your own money or your own security. The more infrastructure that can be put in place to allow the companies to work together, the better, because the companies need help to do that. It won't come naturally. They need to be shown that they are not in competition. Because if they are not shown that they are not in competition they will continue to feel competitive, if that makes sense.

Appendix Four

Summary Tables

Table I:

Summary of key responses

COMPANY	Arad Goch	Fran Wen	Gwent	Iolo	Na n'Og	Spectacle	Clwyd	Powys
ARTISTIC DIRECTOR	Jeremy Turner	Iola Ynyr	Gary Meredith	Kevin Lewis	Geinor Jones	Steve Davies	Tim Baker	Ian Yeoman
TITLE	O Fore Gwyn Tan Nos	Lleisiau yn y Parc	Home Front	Journey	Big Bad Wolf	Where's Andy?	The Mabinogion	Pow Wow
Key Stage Target	1/2	1/2	2/3	1/2	1	1	2	1/2
Pre Workshop	no	yes	no	no	no	yes	yes*	no
Post Workshop	yes	no	no	no	no	yes	yes*	no
Participation	no	no	no	no	no	no	no	yes
Teaching Pack	yes	yes	yes	yes	yes	yes	yes	no
Q&A Session	no	yes	yes	no	yes	yes	yes	no
Specific Links to Curriculum	yes	yes	yes	no	yes	yes	no	no
Devised [D] or Scripted [S]	D/S	S	D	D/S	S	S	D/S	D/S
Number of Performances	99	80	80	40	80	95	40	90
Teacher Involvement	yes	yes	yes	yes	yes	yes	yes	no
Schools Liaison Officer	no	yes	no§	yes	yes	no	yes	no
Funding from L. A. [%]	20	26	18	15	13	10	23	50
Funding from ACW [%]	65	74	80	80	80	80	62	50
Funding from other sources	15	0	2	5	7	10	15	0
Involved in community theatre	yes	yes	yes	no	no	yes	no	yes
Involved in youth theatre	yes	yes	yes	yes	no	yes	no	yes

*Clwyd Theatr Cymru's Theatre for Young People offered a workshop before or after the performance so that children were receiving a day's programme consisting of workshop and performance or vice versa.
§Gwent Theatre did not have a Schools Liaison Officer at the time of interview but were planning to appoint one.

Table II:

Recruitment policies of TIE companies in Wales

Company	TIE experience a criterion for recruitment			Drama experience a criterion for recruitment			Teaching experience a criterion for recruitment			Teaching qualification a criterion for recruitment		
	Essential	Desirable	Not required	Essential	Desirable	Not required	Essential	Desirable	Not required	Essential	Desirable	Not required
Arad Goch			X			X		X				X
Frân Wen			X			X			X			X
Gwent		X			X				X			X
Iolo			X			X			X			X
Na n'Og		X			X				X		X	
Spectacle		X			X			X				X
Clwyd		X				X		X				X
Powys		X				X		X				X

Bibliography

Adland, D. E. (1964), *Group Drama*, London, Longman.

Aldrich, R. (ed.), (1991), *History in the National Curriculum*, London, Institute of Education.

Alington, A. F. (1961), *Drama and Education*, Oxford, Blackwell.

Allen, J. (1979), *Drama in Schools: its Theory and Practice*, London-Exeter, Heinemann.

Arts Council of Great Britain (1992), *Guidance on Drama Education*, London, ACGB.

Arts Council of Wales (2000), *Chronology outlining the Theatre for Young People franchise history*, ACW, Cardiff, http://www.theatr-cymru.co.uk/news/new061000c.htm.

Arts Council of Wales (2001), *Audit of Theatre in Education and Theatre for Young People in Wales*, Cardiff, Cardiff Arts Marketing.

Arts Council of Wales (2002), *The Future of Theatre for Young People in Wales*, ACW, Cardiff.

Assessment Reform Group (2002), *Assessment for Learning*, London, ARG.

Baker, M. (1999), *Arts Council of Wales Response to Theatre in Education Companies Following the Consultation Process*, ACW, Cardiff, http://www.theatr-ymru.co.uk/news/news240399.htm.

Baldwin, P. (2002), A Need for Creative Thinking in *TES* 22nd November.

Barber, M. (1996), *The Learning Game*, Gollancz, London.

Barker, C. (1977), *Theatre Games*, London, Methuen.

Beard, R. M. (1969), *An Outline of Piaget's Developmental Psychology*, London, Routledge.

Best, D. (1992), *The Rationality of Feeling*, London, The Falmer Press.

Boal, A. (1979), trans. Adrian Jackson, *Theatre of the Oppressed*, London, Pluto Press.

Boal, A. (1992), trans. Adrian Jackson, *Games for Actors and Non Actors*, London, Routledge.

Boal, A. (1995), trans. Adrian Jackson, *The Rainbow of Desire*, London, Routledge.

Boal, A. (1998), trans. Adrian Jackson, *Legislative Theatre*, London, Routledge.

Bolton, G. (1979), *Towards a Theory of Drama in Education*, London, Longman.

Bolton, G. (1986), *Selected Writings*, Harlow, Longman.

Bolton, G. (1998), *Acting in Classroom Drama*, Stoke on Trent, Trentham Books.

Bolton, G. & Heathcote, D. (1999), *So You Want to Use Role Play?* Stoke on Trent, Trentham.

Bolton Octagon Theatre-in-Education Company (1975), *Sweetie Pie*, London, Methuen.

British Theatre Guide (2001), *Towards the Provision of a National Theatre for Wales. A Federal System*, British Theatre Guide, http//www.britishtheatreguide. info/articles/130200e.htm.

Brook, P. (1968), *The Empty Space*, London, Penguin.

Bruley, S. (1999), *Women in Britain Since 1900*, Basingstoke, Macmillan.

Byron, K. (ed.), (1962), *DramaDance* 2D, vol. 1, no. 2, Leicester.

Byron, K. (1987), Drama at the Crossroads, Part Two in *DramaDance 2D*, Leicester, vol. 7, no. 1.

Calouste Gulbenkian Foundation [Revised Edition], (1989), *The Arts in Schools*, London, Calouste Gulbenkian Foundation.

Cattanach, A. (1996), *Drama for People with Special Needs*, London, A & C Black.

Clark, B. (1971), *Group Theatre*, Bath, Pitman.

Clifford, S. & Herrmann, A. (1999), *Making a Leap: Theatre of Empowerment*, London, Jessica Kingsley.

Clutty, C. (1992), *Towards a New Education System: The Victory of the New Right*, Lewes, Falmer Press.

Cole, Mike (ed.), (2002), *Professional Values and Practice for Teachers and Student Teachers*, London, David Fulton.

Cook, H. Caldwell (1917), *The Play Way*, London, Heinemann.

Courtney, R. (1968), *Play, Drama and Thought*, London, Cassell.

Cox, B. (1991), *Cox on Cox*, London, Hodder & Stoughton.

Cox, C. B. & Dyson, A. E. (1969), *Fight for Education, A Black Paper*, London, Critical Quarterly Society.

Coxall, B. & Robins, L. (1998), *British Politics Since the War*, Basingstoke, Macmillan.

Craig, S. (ed.), (1980), *Dreams and Deconstructions: Alternative Theatre in Britain*, Ambergate, Amber Lane Press.

Davis, D. (1985), Dorothy Heathcote Interviewed by David Davis in *DramaDance 2D*, vol. 4, no. 2.

Davis, D. (1997), *Interactive Research in Drama in Education*, Stoke on Trent, Trentham Books.

Davis, D. (2001), Geoff Gillham, Obituary in *The Guardian*, 27/7/01, London, Guardian.

Department of Education and Science (1967), *Children and their Primary Schools, The Plowden Report*, London, HMSO.

Department of Education and Science (1967), *Drama: Education Survey 2*, London, HSMO.

Department of Education and Science (1989), *Drama 5–16*, London, HMSO.

Department of Education and Science (1989), *National Curriculum English for Ages 5–16, Proposals of the Secretary of State for Education and Science and the Secretary of State for Wales*, London, HMSO.

Department of Education and Science (1990), *Aspects of Primary Education – The Teaching and Learning of Drama*, London, HMSO.

Department for Education and Skills (2003), *Speaking, Listening, Learning: Working with Children in Key Stages 1 and 2*, Norwich, DfES.

Dodd, N. & Hickson, W. (eds.), (1971), *Drama and Theatre in Education*, London, Heinemann.

Drama (2003), vol. 10, no. 2.

Drama (2003), vol. 11, no. 1.

Drama (2004), vol. 11, no. 2.

Drama Broadsheet (1990), vol. 7, issue 3, Gateshead, NATD.

Emunah, R. (1994), *Acting for Real – Drama, Therapy, Process, Technique and Performance*, New York, Brunner/Mazel.

Equity Wales (1999), *Equity Wales Response to the Proposed New Drama Strategy*, Equity, Cardiff, http:/www.theatr-cymru.co.uk/news/news260299.htm.

Esslin, M. (1984), *Brecht, A Choice of Evils*, London, Methuen.

Esslin, M. (1987), *The Field of Drama*, London, Methuen.

Ewan, F. (1992), *Bertolt Brecht, His Life, His Art, His Times*, New York, Citadel Press.

Fines, J. (1979), Review of Dorothy Heathcote: Drama as a Learning Medium by B. J. Wagner in *London Drama*, vol. 6, no. 1.

Finlay-Johnson, H. (1911), *The Dramatic Method of Teaching*, London, Nisbet.

Fleming, M. (1995), *The Art of Drama Teaching*, London, David Fulton.

Fleming, M. (2001), *Teaching Drama in Primary and Secondary Schools*, London, David Fulton Publishers.

Freire, P. (1972), *Pedagogy of the Oppressed*, Harmondsworth, Penguin.

Gallagher, K. & Booth, D. (2003), *How Theatre Educates*, Toronto, University of Toronto Press.

Green, J. (2001), Peer Education, in *Peer Education. Promotion & Education* VIII(2), j.green@lmu.ac.uk, 2004.

H. M. I. (1989), *A Survey of Theatre in Education in Wales*, Cardiff, Welsh Office.

Halpin, D. (2001), *The Nature of Hope and its Significance for Education*, in British Journal of Educational Studies, vol. 49, no. 4, Oxford.

Head D. (ed.), (1974), *Free Way to Learning*, Harmondsworth, Penguin.

Heathcote, D. (1971), Drama and Education: Subject or System? in N. Dodd & W. Hickson, *Drama and Theatre in Education*, London, Heinemann.

Heathcote, D. (1972), Drama as Challenge in J. Hodgson, *The Uses of Drama*, London, Methuen.

Heathcote, D. (1975), Drama as Education in N. McCaslin (ed.), *Children and Drama*, New York, David McKay.

Heathcote, D. (1980), From the Particular to the Universal in K. Robinson (ed.), *Exploring Theatre and Education*, London, Heinemann.

Heathcote, D. (1980), Material for Meaning in Drama *London Drama*, vol. 6, no. 2, London.

Heathcote, D. (1982), Signs (and Portents?) – the Use of Role for Actors in *SCYPT Journal*, no. 9, London.

Heathcote, D. (1984), Moving into the Drama – an Interview with Geoff Gillham, *SCYPT Journal*, no. 13, London.

Heathcote, D. (1995), Drama as a Process for Change (1976) reprinted in R. Drain, *Twentieth Century Theatre*, London, Routledge.

Heathcote, D. (2000), Contexts for Active Learning in *Drama Research*, vol. 1, London, Heinemann.

Heathcote, D. & Bolton, G. (1995), *Drama for Learning*, Portsmouth, New Hampshire, Heinemann.

Hodgson, J. (1972), *The Uses of Drama*, London, Eyre Methuen.

Hodgson, J. & Banham, M. (1972), *Drama in Education 1, Annual Survey*, London, Pitman.

Hodgson, J. & Richards, E. (1966), *Improvisation*, London, Eyre Methuen.

Holmes, P. & Karp, M. (eds.), (1991), *Psychodrama: Inspiration and Technique*, London, Routledge.

Holt, J. (1984), *How Children Fail*, Harmondsworth, Penguin.

Hornbrook, D. (1989), *Education and Dramatic Art*, Oxford, Blackwell.

Hornbrook, D. (1991), *Education in Drama*, London, The Falmer Press.

Hornbrook, D. (ed.), (1999), *On the Subject of Drama*, Cardiff, OHMCI.

Hornby, R. (1992), *The End of Acting*, Tonbridge, Applause.

Illich, I. (1973), *Deschooling Society*, Harmondsworth, Penguin.

Isaacs, N. (1955), *Some Aspects of Piaget's Work*, London, National Froebel Foundation.

Itzin, C. (1980), *Stages in the Revolution: Political Theatre since 1968*, London, Methuen.

Jackson, T. (1993), *Learning Through Theatre*, London, Routledge.

Jennings, S. (1973), *Remedial Drama*, London, Pitman.

Jennings, S. (ed.), (1987), *Dramatherapy: Theory and Practice for Teachers and Clinicians*, Beckenham, Crook Helm.

Jennings, S. (1990), *Dramatherapy with Families, Groups and Individuals*, London, Jessica Kingsley.

Jennings, S. (ed.), (1992), *Dramatherapy: Theory and Practice 2*, London, Routledge.

Jennings, S. (ed.), (1994), *The Handbook of Dramatherapy*, London, Routledge.

Jennings, S. (ed.), (1998), *Introduction to Dramatherapy*, London, Jessica Kingsley.

Johnson, L. & O'Neill, C. (1984), *Dorothy Heathcote: Collected Writings*, London, Hutchinson.

Johnstone, K. (1981), *Impro*, London, Methuen.

Jones, D. (1985), *Black Book on the Welsh Theatre*, Prilly, Iolo/Bozo.

Jones, G. E. (1997), *The Education of a Nation*, Cardiff, University of Wales Press.

Jones, K. (2003), *Education in Britain 1944 to the Present*, Cambridge, Blackwell.

Jones, R. M. (1972), *Fantasy and Feeling in Education*, Harmondsworth, Penguin.

Kellerman, P. F. (1992), *Focus on Psychodrama*, London, Jessica Kingsley.

Kempe, A. & Nicholson, H. (2001), *Learning to Teach Drama 11–18*, London, Continuum.

Kitson, N. & Spiby, I. (1997), *Drama 7–11*, London, Routledge.

Lawton, D. (1980), *The Politics of the School Curriculum*, London, Routledge and Kegan Paul.

Lawton, D. (1992), *Education and Politics in the 1990s*, London, Falmer Press.

Leach, R. (1970), *Theatre for Youth*, Oxford, Pergamon.

Lester Smith, W. O. (1957), *Education*, Harmondsworth, Penguin.

Light, P. & Littleton, K. (1999), *Social Processes in Children's Learning*, Cambridge, CUP.

Lowenfeld, M. (1969), *Play in Childhood*, Bath, Gollanz.

Male, D. A. (1973), *Approaches to Drama*, London, Allen & Unwin.

Mason, H. & McCall, S. (1997), *Access to Education for Children and Young People*, London, David Fulton.

McCallion, P. (1998), *Achievement for All: Achieving Excellence in Schools*, London, The Stationery Office.

McGrath, J. (1981), *A Good Night Out*, London, Eyre Methuen.

McGregor, L., Tate, M. & Robinson, K. (1977), *Learning Through Drama. Report of Schools Council Drama Teaching Project 10–16*, London, University of London Press.

McLuhan, M. (1967), *The Medium is the Massage*, Harmondsworth, Penguin.

Midwinter, E. (1980), *Schools in Society*, London, Batsford.

Ministry of Education (1949), *Story of a School*, London, HMSO.

Ministry of Education (1954), *Drama in the Schools of Wales*, London HMSO.

Ministry of Education (1963), *Half Our Future, The Newsom Report*, London HMSO.

Morgan, N. & Saxton, J. (1995), Dorothy Heathcote: Educating the Intuition in *Broadsheet. The Drama Education Journal*, vol. 11, London.

Muir, A. (1996), *New Beginnings*, Stoke-on-Trent, Trentham.

Musgrave, P. W. (1975), *The Sociology of Education*, London, Methuen.

National Advisory Committee on Creative and Cultural Education (1999), *All Our Futures*, Sudbury, DFEE.

National Assembly for Wales (2002), *£1.2m for Welsh TIE*, NAW Press Release, Cardiff, http://britishtheatreguide.info/news/welshtie.htm.

National Assembly for Wales (2003), *The Learning Country: The Foundation Phase – 3 to 7 years*, Cardiff, NAW.

Neelands, J. (1998), *Beginning Drama 11–14*, London, David Fulton Publishers.

Neelands, J. & Dobson, W. (2000), *Theatre Directions*, Abingdon, Hodder & Stoughton.

Neill, A. S. (1968), *Summerhill*, Harmondsworth, Pelican.

Northen, S. (2003), Play, in *TES*, 5th May.

Ofsted (1998), *The Arts Inspected*, Oxford, Heinemann.

Ohmci (1998), *Art, Drama and Music in Key Stages 3 and 4*, Cardiff, HMSO.

O'Toole, J. (1976), *Theatre in Education*, Hodder and Stoughton, London.

O'Toole, J. (1992), *The Process of Drama*, London, Routledge.

Paisey, A. (ed.), (1983), *The Effective Teacher*, London, Ward Lock.

Pemberton-Billing, R. & Clegg, J. (1965), *Teaching Drama*, London, University of London Press.

Piaget, J. (1926), translated and revised 1959, *Language and Thought of the Child*, London, Routledge & Kegan Paul.

Pickering, K. (1974), *Drama Improvised*, London, J. Garnet Miller.

Postman, N. & Weingartner, C. (1969), *Teaching as a Subversive Activity*, Harmondsworth, Penguin.

Qualifications, Curriculum & Assessment Authority for Wales (2003), Issue 18, Cardiff, QCAAW.

Redington, C. (1983), *Can Theatre Teach*? Oxford, Pergamon Press.

Research in Drama Education (1996), vol. 1, no. 2, London, RDA.

Research in Drama Education (1997), vol. 2, no. 1, London, RDA.

Research in Drama Education (1998), vol. 3, no. 1, London, RDA.

Research in Drama Education (1999), vol. 4, no. 1, London, RDA.

Richmond, W. K. (1973), *The Free School*, London, Methuen.

Robinson, K. (ed.), (1980), *Exploring Theatre & Education*, London, Heinemann.

Ross, M. (1975), *Schools Council Working Paper 54, Arts and the Adolescent*, London, Evans/Methuen.

Ross, M. (1978), *The Creative Arts*, London, Heinemann.

Savill, C. C. (1988), Theatre-in-Education in Wales in *Planet, the Welsh Internationalist*, no. 67, Aberystwyth, Planet.

Savill, C. C. (1998), On the Acting and Performance Environment in Mid-Wales in *New Welsh Review*, no. 40, spring, Aberystwyth.

Schweitzer, P. (ed.), (1980), *Theatre-in-Education: Four Secondary Programmes*, London, Methuen.

Scott, R. D. (2002), A Giant Among Men, Obituary of John McGrath in *The Sunday Herald* 27/1/02, Glasgow, Sunday Herald.

SCYPT (1983), Journal 11, London, SCYPT.

SCYPT (1984), Journal 12, London, SCYPT.

SCYPT (1984), Journal 13, London, SCYPT.

SCYPT (1986), Journal : New Voices 16, London, SCYPT.

SCYPT (1987), Journal : New Voices 17, London, SCYPT.

SCYPT (1989), Journal : New Voices 18, London, SCYPT.

SCYPT (1990), Journal 20, Porth, SCYPT.

SCYPT (1994), Journal 28, Lancaster, SCYPT.

SCYPT (1995), Journal 30, Lancaster, SCYPT.

Secondary Heads Association (1998), *Drama Sets You Free*, Bristol, Central Press.

Shade, R. (2000), The March of Progress in *Planet No. 139* February/March 2002, Aberystwyth, Planet.

Sharp, P. & Dunford, J. (1990), *The Education System in England and Wales*, London, Longman.

Slade, P. (1954), *Child Drama*, London, Hodder & Stoughton.

Slade, P. (1958), *An Introduction to Child Drama*, London, Hodder & Stoughton.

Slade, P. (1958), *Experience of Spontaneity*, London, University of London Press.

Slade, P. (1966), *Child Drama and its Value in Education*, Birmingham, Educational Drama Association.

Slade, P. (1972), *Drama and the Middle School*, Birmingham, Educational Drama Association.

Slade, P. (date unknown), *Freedom in Education?* Birmingham, Educational Drama Association.

Smith, A. (2003), Roll With It in *Education Guardian*, London, *The Guardian*.

Somers, J. (1994), *Drama in the Curriculum*, London, Cassell.

Speirs, R. (1987), *Bertolt Brecht*, Basingstoke, MacMillan.

Stanislavski, C. (1937), trans. Hapgood, E. J., *An Actor Prepares*, London, Methuen.

Stanislavski, C. (1950), trans. Hapgood, E. J., *Building a Character*, London, Methuen.

Stanislavski, C. (1967), trans. Robbins, J. J., *My Life in Art*, Harmondsworth, Penguin.

Stanislavski, C. (1981), trans. Hapgood, E. J., *Creating a Role*, London, Methuen.

Stanislavski, C. (1990), ed. and trans. Hapgood, E. J., *An Actor's Handbook*, London, Methuen.

Taylor, A-M. (ed.), (1997), *Staging Wales*, Cardiff, University of Wales Press.

Taylor, A-M. (1997), Mapping the Future in *Planet*, vol. 126, December 1997, Planet, Aberystwyth.

Theatre-in-Education Crisis Campaign Steering Group (1994), *For a Full Provision of the Arts for Society and Schools*, London, Campaign Steering Group.

Theatr Powys (1999), *ACW Draft Drama Strategy for Wales: Theatr Powys Response*, Llandrindod, Theatr Powys.

Theatr Powys (2001), *Response to CAM Interim Report on Audit of Theatre in Education and Theatre for Young People in Wales*, Llandrindod, Theatr Powys.

Thomson, P. & Sacks, G. (eds.), (1994), *The Cambridge Companion to Brecht*, Cambridge, Cambridge University Press.

University of Glamorgan (2003), *Press Release 19th November 2003: Planning Theatre's Legacy of Memory*, University of Glamorgan, Pontypridd, http://www.glam.ac.uk/news/releases/ 001364.php.

Wagner, B. J. (1979), *Dorothy Heathcote: Drama as a Learning Medium*, London, Hutchinson.

Warnock, H. M. (1978), *Special Educational Needs*, London, HMSO.

Way, B. (1967), *Development Through Drama*, London, Longman.

Welsh Economy Research Unit (1998), *The Economic Impact of the Arts and Cultural Industries in Wales*, Cardiff, WERU.

Welsh Office (1988), *National Curriculum: A Teacher's Guide*, Cardiff, HMSO.

Whitehead, A. N. (1932), *The Aims of Education*, London, Earnest Benn.

Willett, J. (1964), *Brecht on Theatre*, London, Methuen.

Willett, J. (1977), *The Theatre of Bertolt Brecht*, London, Methuen.

Williams, G. (2002), Drama Teachers on the Cheap in *TES* 22nd November.

Witkin, R. W. (1974), *The Intelligence of Feeling*, London, Heinemann.

Woolland, B. (1993), *The Teaching of Drama in the Primary School*, London, Longman.

Wooster, R. (2006), Paradigm Lost? in *The Journal for Drama in Education*, vol. 22, issue 1, Barnsley, NATD.

Video Sources

BBC (1972), *Three Looms Waiting*, London, BBC.

Bessel, Richard (1994), *Brecht on Stage*, BBC Open University.

University of Newcastle (1997), *What's in Store?* University of Newcastle.

University of Newcastle (2000), *Rolling Role in the National Curriculum*, University of Newcastle.

University of Newcastle (2002), *Pieces of Dorothy*, University of Newcastle.

Abbreviations and Acronyms

ACGB   (Arts Council of Great Britain)

ACW   (Arts Council of Wales)

ASSITEJ   (Association International du Theatre pour l'Enfance et la Jeunesse/ International Association of Theatre for Children and Young People)

BTEC   (Business and Technology Council)

CND   (Campaign for Nuclear Disarmament)

CT   (Children's Theatre)

DIE   (Drama in Education)

ERA   (Education Reform Act)

GCSE   (General Certificate of Secondary Education)

HMI   (Her Majesty's Inspectorate)

INSET   (In Service Training for Teachers)

LEA   (Local Education Authority)

LMS   (Local Management of Schools)

LX   (Electrics [theatre])

NATD   (National Association for Teachers of Drama)

PSE   (Personal and Social Education)

PSHE   (Personal, Social and Health Education)

RE   (Religious Education)

SACRE   (Standing Advisory Council on Religious Education)

SCYPT   (Standing Conference of Young People's Theatre)

SHA   (Secondary Head Teachers Association)

SM   (Stage Manager)

TIE   (Theatre in Education)

WAC   (Welsh Arts Council)

WJEC   (Welsh Joint Education Council)

YPT   (Young People's Theatre)